THICKER *THAN* *Water*

Diary of a Diabetic

R. C. TUTTLE

WESTBOW
PRESS®
A DIVISION OF THOMAS NELSON
& ZONDERVAN

WestBow Press books may be ordered through booksellers or by contacting:

WestBow Press
A Division of Thomas Nelson & Zondervan
1663 Liberty Drive
Bloomington, IN 47403
www.westbowpress.com
1 (866) 928-1240

ISBN: 978-1-5127-0873-8 (sc)
ISBN: 978-1-5127-0874-5 (hc)
ISBN: 978-1-5127-0872-1 (e)

Library of Congress Control Number: 2015913450

Print information available on the last page.

WestBow Press rev. date: 8/27/2015

CONTENTS

The Narrow Gate

PREFACE

The working title for this book was originally *Diary of a Diabetic*. Having experienced some small victories with the disease, I hoped to encourage others. What a *page turner* that would have been. Keeping copies on the shelf probably wouldn't be very difficult. As I wrote, the story became more about my 'rasin' than about my disease. Soon, I realized there wasn't just one story, but many. The words flowed from mind and memory to my fingers on the keyboard; I was thoroughly enjoying the journey.

I spent so much time writing and reminiscing that the title quickly changed to *Hillbilly Proud*. That was more accurate regarding the book's content. And to be honest, it was a much better title than *Diary of a Diabetic*. The story kept evolving until *Hillbilly Proud* became *Thicker than Water*. The book is finished; the story isn't. Real love stories never end…

DEDICATION

Thicker than Water is dedicated to folks who know the difference between: eating dinner and having supper, between cornbread and corn pone, between molasses and blackstrap, between gravy and poor-do, between freckle sop and grease, between pancakes and hoecakes.

It's dedicated to folks: who put out a worsh'n, got their cheeks rosied, had a dose of Hickory Tea, been torn up worse than new ground, carried groceries home in a poke, or walked to the store for a bottle of pop and a jumbo pie.

It is dedicated to folks who can sing *What a Friend We Have in Jesus*, and those who know where Ole Dan Tucker washed his face.

It is dedicated to folks who remember where outdated catalogues ended up.

INTRODUCTION

Therefore comfort each other and edify one
another, just as you also are doing.
1 Thessalonians 5:11 (NKJV)

This book was written to entertain and encourage. There may be readers who recognize themselves in the stories and think, "That's not how I remember it." You might be right. I have tried to be as accurate as memory serves, but memory doesn't always serve. In the course of getting the story told, details may differ in my efforts to recall. Details are important, but not every detail. Some are under the impression that every little detail of their life should be shared with as many as possible. Today's technology comes close to making that happen. However, I wouldn't recommend it.

I admit to being a self-centered person. I would like for everyone to be as fascinated with me and my story as I am. But I'm smart enough to know, that just isn't the case. My siblings will be interested, but they don't really have to read my story because they share so much of it. That's especially true with my sisters who have always been able to read me like a book. We have been separated by distance most of our adult life so when we do get together, it becomes a real gab fest. After thirty minutes of chit chat about what's been going on with them I say, "OK that's enough about you, now let's talk about me. It's a long standing joke regarding my self-centeredness, but the thing that makes a joke funny is the nugget of truth it holds.

With that confession, I'll go on record saying, "There are some things that just don't need to be shared!" No one needs to know every detail of my life or yours. There's room in every closet for a few skeletons. Keep them there; have some secrets. It just might make you more interesting. I'll be sharing numerous stories, but I won't share everything. I hope I've chosen the ones that will entertain and encourage. But, it is not the whole story. I have no intention of sharing that. I have secrets and I will keep them.

THE SUN SHINES BRIGHT

I

HOME IN THE HILLS

My old Kentucky home was and is a place where the sun shines bright. Located across the creek and down the lane, it's where most of my formative years took place. Where you live is not as important as who you live with, but it played an important role in who I became. It was the starting point for my life outside the womb. Who, what, and why I am today was greatly influenced by where I was then. I made it all the way to here, from my old Kentucky home far, far away.

Many years and hundreds of miles separate me from that home, but it remains just a memory away. I physically go back once or twice a year. Emotionally, I go back daily. The older I get, the more often I find myself roaming the hills and valleys of my childhood.

Seeing a bib apron or hair pin can take me back to Granny's room, braiding her hair, listening to Bible stories, or reading Little Golden Books. A walking stick or fly swat can put me back in the garden pulling weeds with Grandpa, or setting on the porch watching him battle the fly population.

Home is where the heart is! Mine has dual citizenship. Most of the time it resides in Texas with the family I gave birth to, but a large portion resides in Kentucky with the family I was blessed to be born into.

It doesn't matter if your home was across the creek, over the bridge, or up the hollow. Eventually, all roads lead home. The roads of our memory can be pleasant to travel or filled with pain. Some are bathed in sunshine and others dark. Thankfully, I learned at an early age to focus on the sun-light. It took a lot longer to focus on the Son's-light.

> For it is the God who commanded light to shine out of darkness, who has shown in our hearts to give the light of the knowledge of the glory of God in the face of Jesus Christ.
> **2 Corinthians 4:6 (NKJV)**

I should have kept that light burning; I would have avoided many falls and stumbling so much in the dark. It took years for the Word to become a lamp unto my feet and a light onto my path. I acted as though God was a flashlight I could pull out of a drawer for emergencies then turn off to keep the battery from running down. I had no idea His battery never ran down.

> The night is far spent, the day is at hand. Therefore let us cast off the works of darkness, and let us put on the armor of light.
> **Romans 13:12 (NKJV)**

Most mornings I awoke sensing the stirrings of life around me. One of the first senses to be aroused was my sense of smell. The aroma of bacon and coffee wafted up the stairs, down the hall and through the bedroom door. That smell told me it was daylight or soon would be. It told me Mom was downstairs in the kitchen and breakfast would soon be on the table.

Our home was in Kentucky, the Bluegrass State, noted for fast horses and beautiful women. The setting was the rural foothills of eastern Kentucky. The farm, the house and outbuildings, including the outhouse, were nestled in a valley between three hills. One on either side with another to the rear provided the backdrop for our old Kentucky home.

I'm not sure why hills are called hills in Kentucky instead of mountains. Maybe there's a maximum height requirement or maybe the term 'Hill-billy' was the deciding factor. In any case, whether hill or mountain, it was picturesque by any standard. Looking back through eyes that have traveled far and seen much, I know those hills to be one of the many beautiful examples of God's creativity.

Beauty surrounded our home in the hills with the exception of January and February. The only way I can describe those Kentucky winters is bleak. The predominant color of the landscape was gray: light, dark, and battleship gray with drab green and splotches of brown. The melting snow created muddy messes outside that got tracked inside. The cold was bitter and biting. How could it not be bleak when the hours of darkness exceeded the hours of daylight?

Even so, there were still some winter days when bleak was blanketed with a layer of glistening snow. Enough snow could turn bleak season into a winter wonderland. Those were days of releasing pent up energy by joyfully romping in the snow. Well, *trying* to romp joyfully in the snow. Not much romping was possible when you were so thickly bundled up.

Going outside meant my little brother and I would be stuffed into snowsuits that radically restricted our movement. Mom spent a lot of time getting us ready; several minutes were spent just searching for the attached mittens that were usually hiding in the sleeves.

Those mittens made it impossible to give fine definition to a snowman's face. That's the reason Frosty had a corn cob pipe, a button nose, and eyes made out of coal. Our Frosty had a mouth, nose, and eyes made out of coal. That's because the coal house was right there in the side yard. Country kids learn to make do with what's available.

One of Mom's favorite sayings was, "Use it up, wear it out, make it do or do without." Since mittens made picking up a button impossible, a chunk of coal would do just fine. Compressing defensive snowballs in those mittens was impossible. We avoided snowball fights for that reason. Plus, the awkward red galoshes on our feet made it difficult to dodge hard packed snowballs.

We spent most of our time riding a sled, a bread pan or a box down the bank by the coal house. Then we would roll around and make snow angels in the yard. When the cold or a snowball to the face sent us rushing inside, Mom spent more time getting us undressed. She invested thirty minutes wrestling us in and out of snowsuits to get fifteen minutes to herself.

When I became a mom, I understood the value of a little peace and quiet. Sometimes fifteen minutes was just long enough to keep me from disciplining to harshly, and it wasn't long enough to pack my bags and run away. Why Mom went to all that trouble became evident when I became a mother.

I took our first son to the pediatrician after an extended vacation at Grandma's house. The doctor asked what his symptoms were. I said. "Well, he doesn't have a fever. He isn't throwing up. He doesn't have a runny nose or a cough. I hope you can tell me what's wrong. He *is* throwing himself out of the crib and being absolutely defiant! If he *isn't* sick, I'm taking him home and beating the living daylights out of him."

The pediatrician laughed, checked him out and said, "Everything looks fine, you've just got yourself a little ringtail tooter. Now, let's talk about better options than beating. There are times when children would be safer, if we could lock parents in the bedroom." He offered great advice that helped me and my three strong willed sons survive their raising.

I defiantly understood mom's need for a few minutes of alone time, and why she went to such great lengths to get it.

II

BEST CHRISTMAS EVER

One of the best days of my childhood involved snow. It was the night before Christmas. Big fluffy flakes had been falling all evening. Granny and middle sis, Good as Gold, were trying to get me and Little Brother settled down for a long winter's nap. They were helping with our Christmas Eve tradition of hanging stockings by the chimney with care. After that, it would be bedtime.

Our Christmas stockings came from Granny. They were those thick cotton 'old lady' stockings that were held up with elastic garters just above the knee. She unwrapped a brand new pair for us every Christmas Eve. They weren't pretty, sparkly, or personalized, but they served the purpose. When Christmas was over and all the goodies emptied, they reverted to their original purpose of keeping Granny's legs warm.

Those stockings could hold: oranges, tangerines, bananas, apples, nuts, candy, a set of jacks, a Christmas coloring book, and (be still oh my heart), a new box of crayons. All of that could be stuffed into *one* of Granny's stockings, *just for me*! Replace the jacks with a toy car or a wooden glider plane and that was usually the contents of my brother's stocking.

That best Christmas ever started with the hanging of those stockings.
We used a small nail or carpet tack and actually hammered them into
the wooden mantle over the fireplace. When defacing the mantle was
complete, it was bedtime. My little brother was on his way to sleep
with Granny downstairs. I was headed into the dreaded dark upstairs
to my little bedroom at the end of the hall. I would be thinking about
the creatures that were stirring up there instead of having sugar
plums dancing in my head.

When out on the porch there arose such a clatter.
We ran for the door to see what was the matter.

Not really sure but we hoped it would be,
Santa arriving with gifts for the tree.

Big Sister stopped us and gave a stern warning.
"If he sees you, there'll be no gifts in the morning!"

Deciding to chance it, we opened the door.
Stepped out, walked around on the snow covered floor.

Then what to our wondering eyes did appear?
Proof positive Santa had already been there!

We saw tracks in the snow from reindeer hoofs,
with imprints of sleigh on our porch, not the roof.

Presents were left in store shopping bags,
none of them gift wrapped; all had price tags.

The most wonderful Christmas, an astonishing night,
for Santa had almost been caught in our sight.

Behind the scenes, Dad had retrieved the gifts hidden in a big wooden
tool chest in the garage. It was a detached garage a short distance

from the house and because the snow kept falling, he decided to put the presents on the porch instead of making the trek later. When he came up the front steps loaded with packages, he slipped and fell.

That's what caused such a clatter. And, his slide marks provided the imprints we thought were left by sleigh runners. The reindeer tracks were made by our dog, Old King. He was part boxer, part bulldog and had been walking around the snow covered porch. I'm sure he danced and pranced around Daddy when he fell. As we got older and reminisced about that Christmas, we learned that Good as Gold delayed our sprint for the door just long enough for Daddy to drop the gifts and run.

I was convinced Santa had so many houses to visit, he only had time to fly through our wrap around porch and drop off the presents. If sister hadn't tried to stop us, we would have actually seen that jolly old elf. Thinking it over the next day, we were glad she stopped us; she might have been right. If we had seen him, he might not have left the gifts and we would not have gotten to stay up late playing with them. Plus, we still had all those stocking goodies on Christmas morning.

Could it possibly get any better? **Yes it could!** My little brother got a wagon! I wasn't even bummed out about getting a doll to carry around when he got a red wagon to carry him around. That's because my parents made a bed for me in his new wagon and I got to sleep downstairs in Granny's room too. She had a fireplace in her bedroom which kept the creatures from stirring all night long and I slept warm, safe, and secure.

Instead of waking up to breakfast smells, I woke up to the aroma of celery, onions, and turkey cooking. Mom's Christmas dinner preparations had started. Forget the Cratchits and the Waltons, it was all about the Cline Christmas that year. I'm not sure Norman Rockwell could have captured a better picture of holiday bliss.

Topping off the best Christmas ever, my stocking had a box of crayons with a white Crayola for the first time ever. That meant I could color the fur around Santa's suit and the ball at the end of his hat! Until then, I had to leave those items uncolored. The coloring book pages were printed on that old rough unbleached paper; the white crayon added just enough contrast to make a tinge of white better than leaving it blank.

III

THE SEASONS

Christmas was the best thing about Kentucky winters. There were a few other days when winter wasn't so bad. Those were the days we got to make snow ice cream; we called it snow cream. Milk, sugar, vanilla, and lots of snow was the recipe for a big bowl of instant brain freeze. Sphenopalatine ganglioneuralgia to be exact. Why would I know that? Let me assure you that I did not want to know that term. In fact, I'm pretty sure no one needs to know it.

You see, my youngest son takes perverse pleasure in making me learn ridiculous things that I have absolutely no use for. It's some sort of payback for me having to push, pull, and drag his extremely bright self through every phase of his education from first grade through his associate's degree. Now he loves learning and won't stop quizzing me on things I do not need to know or have an interest in learning! In this instance, he would not relent until I could pronounce the scientific term for brain freeze.

Even if I become a contestant on Jeopardy, the odds of this word showing up are astronomical. That's why I'm taking this, most likely, only opportunity to use it. Knowledge is a terrible thing to waste. Maybe?

As I was saying, Kentucky winters improved with snow cream. Several spoons would be digging into the bowl at the same time. That made it necessary to take really big bites in order to get your fair share. The cost of really big bites was brain freeze.

I never understood why, but we had to wait until the second snow of the season before Mom would make snow cream. There was some reference about the first snow not being clean enough, as if it came from somewhere other than the sky! I didn't pay much attention to that rule; as long as the snow wasn't yellow or covered with coal dust, I ate some.

When Kentucky winters gave way to spring, the lane to the house and the path leading to the fields out back were edged with thousands of daffodils. The yellow blossoms and bright green leaves pushed *bleak season* to the background. Soon the bulbs Mom planted in the fall were blooming, and the walkway to the front porch was outlined with crocus and tulips. Several spots of purple could be seen from iris plants that returned year after year.

Flowers were everywhere. We had so many daffodils, we could pick as many as we wanted. Vases, bowls, and jars of them filled our home in spring. We called them Easter flowers but most often, they showed up before the bunny, the bonnets and the colored eggs. However, there were a few times Easter was so early, we went to church in the snow. It wasn't a nice egg hunt, but we still got to show off our Easter dresses, hats, gloves and obligatory patent leather shoes.

I have a vague idea of when Easter is celebrated each year, but I am happy to leave the calculations in the capable hands of the calendar folks. Although usually in April, it can occur the end of March or the first of May. I was born on Easter Sunday, and I can't remember my birthday ever falling on Easter. I'm sure it has in the past few decades, but that would not be my preference. I avoid competitions I don't have a chance of winning. Can you imagine your birthday competing with the Resurrection of Christ! February 29th, the Fourth of July or December 25th would be better than Easter.

No matter if it fell in March, April or May, Easter signaled the day we could officially and fashionably start wearing white. We were country, but we had fashion rules. It wasn't proper to wear white before Easter or after Labor Day. That was the rule and we followed it. There were some folks secure enough not to care about the fashion rules; I salute them. However, that's not usually the case with young girls. We wouldn't risk being ridiculed by uppity folks.

Uppity folks are those who look down their noses at others. It's usually the only way they have of elevating themselves. Let's be honest, uppity has nothing to do with economic status. You don't have to live on a hill to look down your nose at others. Some folks spend too much time up on Snob Knob.

> For I say, through the grace given to me, to everyone
> who is among you, not to think of himself more
> highly than he ought to think, but to think soberly,
> as God has dealt to each one a measure of faith.
> **Romans 12:3 (NKJV)**

This verse helps me slide down Snob Knob when vanity starts to take over. If am not on guard, a haughty attitude in others can very quickly rub off on me. I keep Mom's paraphrase of this verse handy for quick recall, *don't' start getting too big for your britches*. It helps me stay off the hill of haughtiness.

Spring in Kentucky started with Dogwood blooming quickly followed by the purple Redbud trees. That precursor to summer ended with pink Mountain Laurel in glorious array on deep green hillsides. By July, the lush green lawns had patches of white clover, purple wood violets and yellow dandelion. Honey bees buzzed from clover to clover and flower to flower, then made their way to the bee hives beside the coal house.

There was such a variety of nectar for the bees, we always had honey for our biscuits. Just chewing on the comb was a special treat. The old folks could look at a jar of honey and tell what flowers were used to make it just from the color. When it was time to rob the hives, Dad and Grandpa wore big screened hats and carried smokers to run the bees out so they could harvest the honey.

The 'bee busy' lawn of summer was accented with red and pink rose bushes that had such long and flower laden branches, a natural arch formed around the center bush. It was a great smelling retreat for day dreaming or playing hide and seek. Big blue holly hocks stood by the well with bell shaped flowers that were a whir of humming bird activity. We tried to catch the tiny birds, but no matter how far they flew into the blossoms, we were never quick enough.

White hydrangeas, snowball bushes to us, lined the side of the smokehouse and steps leading down to the cellar. A low rock wall separated the back yard from the vegetable garden and was lined with tall larkspurs of pink and blue with marigolds underneath. On the top of the wall, at the edge of the garden, there were leaf lettuce beds. In the corner grew rhubarb plants of red and green with elephant ear shaped leaves. Bold and beautiful blossoms of pink peonies were on display in the side yards.

Pee-own-ees, in our native tongue, were the 'go to' flowers for arrangements. They were much in demand for Memorial Day/ Decoration Day. That's when the family graveyard was manicured and the graves decorated with flowers. Most families had graveyards on their property and floral tributes were used to honor deceased love ones. Mom made the arrangements from flowers grown in her garden. There always seemed to be an abundant supply of peonies for her to use.

Decoration Day signaled the beginning of summer. Those days were spent outside from daylight until dark and barefoot, even with those pesky bees lighting in the grass. Granny had a rule of *no bare feet* until May. Evidently hillbillies wouldn't catch a cold if they waited until then to kick off their shoes. I don't think I ever abided by that rule. I did abide by her rule *no wading in the creek* until 'dog days' passed. I never knew what 'dog days' were; I just knew it sounded a lot more serious than catching a cold.

There was a big creek flowing at the front of our property and a small stream (branch) by the side of our house. Both provided lots of fun and entertainment. We all used the swimming hole and my brothers fished, gigged, and trapped in the big creek. My little brother and I waded and caught crawdads in the branch.

I didn't really do any catching, my brother caught and I assisted by flipping over the rocks where crawdads hid. He was brave enough to grab them behind their pinchers. They didn't provide enough food or fun for me to risk getting pinched. I would have taken a chance, if the little creatures had candy on their tail instead of a tasteless piece of meat.

I tried to obey most of the rules: No snow cream from the first snow, no white shoes before Easter, no bare feet before May, and no wading during 'dog days'. It might have been easier to obey the rules, if there had been good reasons for them. I needed explanations.

I was the 'why' girl. Why couldn't I go to the barn when animals were being born? Why would they be scared of me, if they weren't scared of adults? Why do we need a flogging rooster when the hens lay the eggs? And greatest mystery of all, why are bugs that come out in July, called June Bugs? Some things just didn't make much sense.

June Bugs were big green florescent beetles. They provided hours of entertainment in **July**. We caught them, tied a string around their hind leg and let them fly here and yon. City kids walked their dogs, country kids walked June Bugs. Another entertaining insect of summer was lightning bugs. They flickered all over yards, fields and hills. Evenings were spent watching and catching lightening bugs (fireflies). We put them in jars to make country night lights. They only emitted just enough light to see the bug itself, but they were fun to watch and could put you to sleep quicker than counting sheep.

When sultry summers grew hot and stifling, I knew my favorite season would be coming soon. Cooler breezes started bringing the thermometer down and autumn was gently blown into the hills and valleys. October foliage blazed with burgundy, orange and gold. Leaves would start falling and by the time they crunched under your feet, the air was crisp and refreshing.

IV

PRIVILEGE HAD A PRICE

I realize now what a privilege it was to wake up and be raised in that country setting. I'm sure my siblings feel the same, but the privilege had a price. The price was hard work, lots and lots of hard work. We raised almost everything we needed and since I don't recall lacking for necessities, someone must have been working very hard. The price of privilege was higher for the five older siblings than for me and Little Brother. The highest price was paid by our parents.

Every day began at the break of dawn. That's why I woke up sensing the stirrings of life around me. The second sense to kick in was my sense of hearing. The rooster crowed, cows mooed, doors opened, gates creaked, and the well bucket clanged. I could hear bits and pieces of hushed conversations coming from the room my sisters shared next door.

The boy's room was down the hall. I did not like the boy's room. With only one window, it always seemed dark and had an even darker closet. One section of the bedroom wall pulled out for access to the creepy attic above the kitchen. My older brothers and sisters shared rooms. Mine was at the end of the hall over the porch; a creaky swing hung from the ceiling below. It was a tiny room, just big enough to hold one little bed and one little frightened girl, me.

When I awoke in my little room, I would start squirming and stretching in bed. No matter the weather, if it was still dark, I was usually under the cover. That's because cover was my third line of defense against monsters. Ask any child, sleeping with someone is the first line of defense, light is the second line of defense and head under the cover is the third line of defense. If you can't see the monsters, the monsters can't see you.

My third line of defense ran the gambit from Double Wedding Ring and Dutch Girl heirlooms to old pieced together scrap quilts. Many were made by my mother and many were handed down from grandmothers. I appreciated quilts for more than just their defensive capabilities. I was intrigued with where some of the quilt pieces came from. Had they been bought at the store? Were they cut from worn out clothing, or were they just scraps of feed sacks? In some cases they were both.

That's because back then, much of our haute couture originated in the saddle house/feed room of the barn. When I got older, I competed with my sisters to *call dibs* on pretty feed sacks. When we finished using the cattle feed they contained, the empty sacks were used for fabric. We made skirts, dresses and quilts from feed sacks.

When who called dibs became an issue, we resorted to taking turns. If 'quilt sack' was called, that meant the material was too ugly for clothing. I used 'quilt sacks' when granny taught me how to piece my first quilt square. It was a beginner's Nine Patch. Some of the ugliest feed sacks made some of the prettiest quilts.

On cold mornings I would soak up warmth from my quilt cocoon. It was part of my morning ritual and preparation for the cold. In winter, it was not uncommon to see your breath in the frigid air upstairs. Sleeping upstairs in the cold and putting bare feet on the linoleum floor was why I never had trouble ignoring Granny's 'no bare feet before May' rule. I had been conditioned all winter long to go barefoot way before May arrived.

Mornings were a wondrous time for me because **I did** wake up, and because I was still there in my old Kentucky home. Monsters had not carried me off to some nether region during the night; I was still alive.

Daddy worked for the railroad and was away several days at a time, then home for several days in a row. Being number six of seven children meant I had to sleep upstairs when Daddy was home. My younger brother, *the baby*, slept downstairs with Mommy when Daddy was away. He took my spot in Granny's bed, when Dad was home.

What is it with the babies of the family? My older siblings say that in our family, the baby girl and the baby boy were spoiled. I'll admit we had it easier than they did. Mom and Dad had a little more time and a little more money for us. However, I don't think getting indoor plumbing, a telephone and a bedroom by yourself equates to being spoiled. But, I could be wrong.

I considered the possibility when two of my older siblings introduced me to an old friend of theirs. We were adults at that time, and paying respects at a funeral home visitation. I can't remember who died; I remember the conversation. They said, "Old Friend, this is our baby sister, I'm sure you remember her." Without missing a beat Old Friend reached to shake my hand and said, "Hello there Brat, how are you doing?" It was obvious he remembered me. And yes, I got the message loud and clear; I might have been a little spoiled. But since I was not THE baby of the family, I'm going to weigh in on the subject.

My mom gave preferential treatment to the boys. That was under-standable where Daddy was concerned, head of the house, love of her life and all. That's as it should be in a healthy marriage. I even understood my older siblings having some perks I didn't due to their age. But the pecking order should have stopped with the baby, not with me. I had absolutely no one to peck.

Mom gave all kinds of preferential treatment to my little brother. How he managed to become such a good man is a mystery to me. I could understand the sleeping arrangements, but having to pretend he was the winner of every family competition, really?

The best example was *Dragnet*. "Just the facts Ma'am, just the facts." Remember how the show opened with Joe Friday's introduction to the crime? "It was a (whatever day of the week)." My family gathered around the TV before the episode began and tried to guess what day of the week the crime occurred. No matter who guessed the right day, we had to tell The Baby he won. We couldn't upset the baby you know. We, meaning Mom wouldn't let us upset the baby. I can only speak for myself; it wouldn't have bothered me if he got upset.

When he was older and shouldn't have been babied, he still was. I could wake up sick and running fever. As long as I wasn't broken out with a childhood disease, Mom would say, "You should probably toughen it out and go on to school." I did. When Little Brother said, "I don't feel good," she said, "You might be coming down with something, you better stay home." He did. Maybe it had something to do with me needing school more than any of my smarty pants, grade skipping siblings, but I doubt it.

Once I got my own baby to…well, baby, I understood my mom's motivation. Being a first time mom, I rushed for success. It was about my child exceeding expectations and averages. It was about walking, talking, feeding himself by a certain age. It was overachievement and worry. Forty percent was worry he might not develop on schedule and sixty percent worry that I would not show well in the mother competition.

First time moms often allow their own mothers, mothers-in-law, friends and neighbors to determine the length of their child's baby stage. All it takes to get us in the 'Hurry Up' mode is a few conversations with emphases added: "Are you *still* breast feeding?" "My children were *potty trained by* ..." "He *isn't* crawling *yet?*" "He sure has an *attachment* to his 'fill in the blank,' mother, bottle, blanket, pacifier."

When consecutive children come along, we rush for convenience; time and attention has to be divided. We push them to do more for themselves so we can do more THINGS, like laundry, cleaning and cooking. When the baby arrives, we realize how many precious moments were lost rushing. Feeling guilty, we slow down and hold on for as long as the baby lets us.

My baby's older brothers think he had it easy. He did. But *my* baby and his brothers, like my sister's boys and my mother's boys, managed to become wonderful men in spite of their mom's mistakes or their birth order. Birth order plays a role in who we become, but whether oldest, middle, or the baby, there are positives and negatives associated with each position.

There were seven children in our family. I occupied the sixth slot. I had a position, but finding my place was quite difficult. I didn't have to work very hard for anything except attention. To this day, the one place I cannot be taken, is **for granted**. By the time I started searching for a place, all the good slots had been taken. There was brains, beauty, hunters, and athletes, then my little brother came along and filled the baby slot. I didn't fit any of the molds. I needed something that was unique to me.

I wasn't as smart, as good, as talented, or as pretty as any of them. There were no athletic opportunities for girls, I had no talent for music, and there was no time or resources for dance classes or gymnastics. I chose to ride horses, jump out of barn lofts, climb trees and get attention by being a rough and tough tomboy.

Mom often cautioned me to stop competing with the neighbor-hood boys or I'd never find a husband. She was wrong. I found one who has been by my side for forty three years. I didn't intimidate him because he doesn't intimidate easily. I'll admit by junior high, I started letting some of the boys win; by high school, most of the boys were strong enough to win. That was okay because by then, I was only interested in the ones who were braver or smarter than me.

Most of my motivation came from Daddy. I got on a skittish horse one day and the horse's owner gave Dad a surprised look. He said, "She's fearless. If you can saddled it, she'll try to ride it." Courageous would have been a better description because I was not fearless. I had lots and lots of fears; courage just became my weapon of choice in battling them. Daddy's approval made the battle worth it, so I became courageous. Dad once told a doctor worried about me passing out, "She wouldn't faint if you cut her arm off."

That's what Daddy thought, and I spent most of my childhood trying to prove him right. Both of my parents were great motivators. Mom's style was the opposite of Dad's. It wasn't negative, just different. I was a boundary pusher. The girl with the distinction of being, 'the one who gave Mom more trouble than all the other children put together'. I did give her lots of trouble, but more than **all** the others put **together**? Mom and I were alike in so many ways; it made our differences more intense.

We butted heads often. It usually boiled down to my wanting her to like me and her wanting me to be like my sisters. She already had Perfection and Good as Gold for daughters. She had no idea who I was and seemed fearful of what I would become. I think she assumed because she had been so blessed with my sisters, I was bound to turn out bad by default. Even that became motivational for me; I needed to prove Daddy right and Mom wrong. So, even my conflicts with Mom were beneficial.

I got the very things I needed for success and happiness from both parents. Daddy believed I could do anything I put my mind to, and Mom thought I always needed taken down a peg or two. She was right about that, I do have a tendency to get 'a little too big for my britches' every now and then.

My son, hear the instruction of your father, and do not forsake the law of your mother; For they will be a graceful ornament on your head, And chains about your neck.
Proverbs 1:8-9 (NKJV)

Mom and I had our last head butting after I became a parent. I was visiting her with my first born and being a bit picky with his food and schedule. She said, "Rhonda Jean!" Oh no…she used my middle name, I'm in trouble! "I think you're just starting to get above your raisn, young lady." I didn't think concern for what was in the best interest my child qualified as the actions of a snob. But, I suppose her occasionally taking me down a peg or two probably helped me stay off the hill of haughtiness.

Mom said I was the 'hard headest young'un' she ever seen. She was wrong! Just so you know, I have paid for my raisn and pay back has been a pain in the…heart. As a matter of fact, it has been a pain in very part of my body; it just usually settles in my heart. I have three sons. If you look up Hard Headed Young'un in the encyclopedia, my picture is still there. But, only because **all three** of them emphatically REFUSED to have their picture taken for the distinction.

V

LITTLE GIRL FEARS

I was not the baby of the family, but too young to stay up late. Dad sent me to bed first, in the dark, by myself. I had to be brave or risk looking weak in Daddy's eyes; I wasn't about to let that happen! For most of my life, the opinion that mattered most to me was his. I feared him with the reverent fear I now have for God. I'm not lifting Dad up to god status, or lowering God to human status. I'm simply saying it's easier to trust your heavenly father as an adult when you had a wonderful earthly father as a child. So every night at bedtime, I practiced becoming something I wasn't, brave.

I would take that slow, steady walk across the living room with my heart pounding in my chest and ears. Reaching the bottom of the stairs, I would look up into a vast and scary darkness. My foot touched the first step, and my mind began repeating, "Do not flail your arms around searching for the light." Halfway up, I'd remind myself again, "You can't disappoint Daddy; he can still see you from below."

I would continue, "Just three more steps, just two more, just one more." I knew exactly which step had to be reached before my frantic search could begin. On the fourth step from the top, the circling arm motion started. "Where's the string? Nothing yet. What if I hit some 'thing' in the dark? What if some 'thing' hits me? What if the bulb is burned out?"

I'd take another step. "Don't pull too hard; the string might break. You can't reach the short chain. Can I reach it from the banister?" Reach, circle, and reach! "Aha, there's my life line!" Light was my only protection until I reached the covers on the bed.

Daddy never told me I had to be brave; I just knew he expected it. I also knew Daddy could protect me from anything, if he was there. I just wasn't sure he could get upstairs quicker than monsters could pull me beyond the press or under a bed to the nether regions. I didn't know where 'beyond' or 'nether regions' were; I just knew they were somewhere. If I disappeared, would my family know where to look? My only hope was Granny. Maybe she would know where to start the search.

Granny knew a lot of mysterious things. She knew about giants, about a man swallowed by a whale, and about babies sent down streams in baskets. I was always on the lookout for babies floating in the swimming hole or the pond in front of the old Allen place. That pond had lots of reeds and cattails like the pictures in my Bible storybook. I looked, but never found a basket or a baby. Granny even knew when God got mad. That was when He destroyed everything with a flood.

Every time it rained for several days, I thought God was mad. Once I got so upset I started crying while sitting on the couch beside Daddy. When he asked what was wrong, I told him my side was hurting. I didn't want him to know I was afraid. That was the first lie I remember telling him. Dad rubbed my side for a long time that night. I calmed down and thought, maybe dying wouldn't be so bad if Dad was with me.

There are many valuable things Dads can leave as an inheritance for their children, but nothing is more important than security. Real security comes by introducing them to their Heavenly Father at an early age so they will never have to be alone.

> "Have I not commanded you? Be strong and of good courage; do not be afraid, nor be dismayed, for the Lord your God is with you wherever you go."
> **Joshua 1:9 (NKJV)**

I don't know if Granny told me about the rainbow at the end of the flood or about God's promise to never destroy the earth with water again. I was focused on the fear. I'm glad she didn't tell me about Sodom and Gomora because that would have triggered all kinds of anxiety when forest fires hit the hills.

When I was old enough to really understand the Noah story, I loved the rain. I would sit on the porch swing reveling in the storms. The point I intended to make was this, Granny had God connections. She knew about mysterious things and probably had a good idea where the nether regions were.

We never talked about the danger I faced at night, but I knew that she knew. She wouldn't have taught me that special prayer if she didn't know. Just in case the worst happened, she armed me with this: *Now I lay me down to sleep, I pray the Lord my soul to keep,* ***IF I SHOULD DIE*** *before I wake, I pray the Lord, my soul to take!* That prayer was all the proof I needed; Granny knew about the danger.

It was obvious she loved me, that's why I didn't understand her not mentioning the danger I was in to Daddy. Maybe he would start sending all of us to bed at the same time. There was safety in numbers. How was it possible that Daddy, who knew almost everything, didn't know monsters only took children, if they were alone?

All it would really take would be sending my big brother upstairs with me. He was brave and could turn on the light to make sure I was safe under the cover before coming back down. Wouldn't that be the trifecta of protection? I would have Big Brother, light, and cover. Unfortunately, that didn't happen. I guess no one wanted Daddy to think they were afraid, even Granny.

When each morning came and I did awake, I celebrated with stretching and squirming. Then I would uncover my head and take big breathes of fresh air. The celebration didn't last long because Mom would call me down to breakfast. I would have gone down anyway. My older brothers and sisters were usually up and at'em before me and I was up there alone again. If it was daylight, I'd take my time and do an 'in your face monster' leisurely stroll downstairs.

However, if I had to go down before daylight, the walk began with a running jump from the middle of my bed to outside the doorway. Pretty crafty move for a little girl, right? I knew the smart thing was never letting your legs to dangle over the side of the bed, just in case. Once the leap was made, I sprinted down the hall toward the dreaded press. At the top of the landing, in front of that door, I reached out and grabbed the banister post at the top of the stairs. Then I immediately flipped my body around the corner with a maneuver that would have gotten a pat on the back from Bela Karolyi.

After sticking a 9.2 landing on the fourth step from the top, I ran like greased lightning down to the light, to people and protection. I was always being scolded for being loud and rambunctious, but that was a small price to pay for being alive. I was downstairs and invincible until bedtime came again.

VI

DADDY

I wasn't completely invincible of course. There was always a chance I would get sent to the cellar when something was needed to cook for supper. Usually it was for potatoes which were stored low and within my reach. Getting potatoes and onions was worse than getting canned goods. A large portion of the summer harvest was stored in the cellar. Irish potatoes, sweet potatoes, and onions were in large bins. Canned goods were on deep wooden shelves which were arranged by type of food and size of the canning jar.

Pints, quarts, half gallons and a few gallon jars followed in sequence from front to back. Big jars of fruits and vegetables were necessary because there were a lot of mouths to feed. The big jars were too far back for me to reach; the older siblings had to get them from the scary back rows.

Our cellar wasn't under the house like a basement. It was under the smoke house located out back. You had to go down steps outside of the smoke house to get to the cool, earthy smelling concrete cellar. Did I mention it was dark and scary down there? For light, you had to leave the door propped open because it had a creepy way of closing on its' own. I had seen eyes down there and I don't mean on the potatoes.

I didn't feel invincible in the cellar and tried to steer clear of the kitchen when dinner preparations started. But needing to be in the thick of the action, I often got caught 'handy' to get something from the cellar. My defense system was singing loudly on the way down the steps, then giving a swift kick to the door before removing the pin and pulling back the clasp.

That was my 'coming in' warning so whatever lurked down there could hide, crawl in a hole, or slither under shelves. I didn't like surprises; I didn't want to see 'whatever' and I hoped 'whatever' did not want to see me.

Some of the farm chores were better than others, and some were actually fun. Two favorites were riding the hay rake with Daddy and sitting on the drag when newly plowed ground had to be smoothed out. Little Brother and I also enjoyed being hay compactors.

When it was time to gather hay. The old blue Studebaker pick-up was driven to the fields with me, my brother, and his neighborhood friend sitting on top of the cab. The men pitched hay in the bed of the truck and we would jump around to pack it down. When it couldn't hold any more, we made burrows in the hay riding back to the barn. When the loose hay was being pitched into the barn loft, we swung from ropes over the rafters and dropped into the big piles until the next run was made.

Hoeing corn was not fun, but it was better than going to the cellar. When the big field needed hoeing, all of us were expected to work. Dad even made short hoes for my little brother and me. We tried to keep up with the grownups, but the faster we went, the more plants we cut down.

Not wanting to get called out, we took even more time sticking cut plants back in the ground and propping them up with dirt. I'm sure it only took a couple of days before we were busted by all the dead plants, but Daddy never said anything. I guess he felt giving us a good work ethic was more important than a few ears of corn.

Rounding up horses was a downright scary chore. Old Bill just knew when Daddy was going to plough. On those days, if he wasn't kept in his stall the night before, he refused to go in on work mornings. He just ate standing in the hall and stretched his head though the door to his feed trough.

When he finished eating, he headed for the hills. That's when Daddy used the family as a mobile corral. That chore taught me to pray, not the 'Lay Me Down' kind for my soul at night. These were prayers that could only come from standing on a hillside with a huge horse galloping toward you.

"Dear God, please don't let him break through my section. If I'm not brave, Daddy will be disappointed. Send him toward Big Brother, Amen." Truthfully, I would have been okay with the horse heading for Little Brother, not that I harbored him any ill will. All of us probably had some sibling rivalry to varying degrees, but BLOOD IS THICKER THAN WATER; we looked out for each other in most cases. In the corral case, I figured if the baby chickened out, he wouldn't get scolded. I didn't want to disappoint Daddy or get scolded for letting the horse get away.

I'm sure my little brother didn't want that either, but it didn't seem to matter as much to him as it did to me. I know he respected Daddy and cared about his opinion; he just never seemed to need Dad's approval as badly as the rest of us. Observing my little brother as an adult, I realize how much he is like Daddy, quiet, strong, and not easily swayed by the opinions of others.

Stoic would be a good description of Daddy. My uncle, Dad's little brother, told me he never wanted to disappoint Daddy when they were growing up. He said he always tried to do things perfectly when working with him because he always felt lacking by comparison. Those who loved Daddy didn't want to let him down and those who knew him desired his good opinion.

Coming home one night, I asked a date if he would like to come in for a while. He said, "Well, that depends on whether your Dad is home or not." I asked why all the boys were so afraid of Daddy and he said, "Because your daddy is the kind of man who goes bear hunting with a switch!"

I had never heard that saying and burst out laughing. It was funny, but not much of an exaggeration.

It was easy to see how Dad could leave that kind of impression. But as I got older, I had the opportunity to see his soft side every now and then. It was apparent in the way he treated his family and his friends. He was compassionate with Mom and all of us kids when we were sick or hurt, and he was generous to those in need.

Daddy loved his family. I knew I was loved at a very early age, not from being told, but from being shown. Daddy worked for the C&O Railroad. His paycheck provided the things we needed that he couldn't coax from the ground by the sweat of his brow. I never saw him idle except on Sundays. If there was daylight, there was work to be done and everyone in our family had responsibilities according to their capabilities.

On hot summer days, my responsibility was taking water to the 'menfolk' working in the field. For a little girl, that chore was more of a privilege than work. About mid-morning Mom would fill a big jug with ice water, wrap a kitchen towel around it, and have me take it to the field. The dish towel kept the jar insulated and kept it from slipping out of my hands when the condensation started.

I wanted to do a good job; my progress was plodding and deliberate. I held that jar so tightly my arms and tummy were freezing by the time I got to the field. The melting ice kept a tinkling rhythm on the sides of the jar and provided an accompaniment to my small steps.

When I got near the field, Dad would look up with steel blue eyes, a rare smile and say, "Hey, hey, here comes our water girl." With an upward motion of his arm, he'd wipe the sweat from his face and push his well-worn cap to the back of his head. I would hand the water up and stand in the shade of his shadow to watch him drink. I could tell he needed and appreciated my efforts.

After everyone quenched their thirst, work continued and my job was over until the next hot work day and the water girl was needed again. I would put the jug under a tree and walk back down the path a lot faster and little taller. It was a small task, but one that was necessary. Knowing I could help gave me a sense of duty and germinated my understanding of love.

Daddy worked alone when my older brothers were in school. At those times, Mom sent me to the field with a smaller and much easier to manage jug of water. After Daddy finished drinking, the jug and I went to the shade of the apple tree. I would sit on the fresh plowed ground and scrunch my toes through the hot crusty top soil down to the cool dirt below. As I played my hot and cold toe games, I watched big drops of sweat fall from the tip of Daddy's nose. He would get so wet with perspiration, only his pant legs remained dry. Almost every second a big drop of sweat fell to the ground and I would count the drops, as high as my capabilities allowed.

The shade of that tree was where my understanding of love took root. I learned at an early age love was an action word. Dad loved us because he worked so hard to provide for us. He was a man of few words; I think that was because his actions spoke so eloquently, he didn't need many.

VII

ALMOST INVINCIBLE

Other than whatever was in the cellar and the horse on the hill, I was almost invincible in daylight. Unless…there might be a small chance a giant was living in the valley beyond the barn. Granny told me about one who was killed by a shepherd boy a long time ago. I couldn't rule out the possibility that giants might be like snakes, if there's one, there's probably another. That's why I steered clear of that area except when it was hog butchering time.

I felt pretty safe then because it usually occurred Thanksgiving weekend when lots of folks were around. Hogs and turkeys had more to worry about than I did at that time of year. I wanted to explore beyond the valley, but I needed a sling shot like the shepherd boy. My big brother had one. If he would make one for me and teach me how to use it, I could practice and do some exploring on my own. That would make me seem more fearless to Dad!

Yes sir, I was almost invincible in daylight. I knew how to avoid the flogging rooster by being fast enough to reach the porch before he could reach me, and I took the precaution of never going through the barn gate without an adult. That kept me from getting gored by the bull.

Oh sure, cows had horns too, but they weren't as dangerous as a bull. I wasn't as scared of the cows because another chore of mine was holding the cow's tail when my parents milked. I was more afraid of the cow kicking me than goring me. Besides, have you ever looked at a cow's eyes, they are peaceable critters. Bulls might be in the same family, but look at their eyes; bulls are mean. Cows sniff and leisurely move along. Bulls huff, paw the ground, and lower their head in a menacing way.

Holding the cow's tail was another small, but important job. If it swished in the milk pail, the milk had to be thrown out. Throwing out an entire pail of milk was not economical. We drank milk like it was water. When the cows calved in the spring, we had to drink store bought milk. That's because the cow's entire supply went to the new calf.

We didn't like store bought milk and were happy when the calves were finally weaned! Then we could enjoy fresh sweet milk plus, thick churned buttermilk and homemade butter. I'm not sure which I liked best, fresh churned butter on hot crusty cornbread, or hot crusty cornbread in fresh churned buttermilk.

The only thing left to interfere with my daylight invincibility was the **booger man.** It was my understanding he could show up at anytime, anywhere! Don't let the name confuse you, we had a booger man instead of a bogeyman. Both were used to scare little children, but there were differences between the two, at least in my mind.

A bogeyman was red, had horns, a pointed tail, a pitchfork, and was covered in flames. The booger man was green and covered in… well, he's the **booger** man. I don't think that's the picture Mom and Granny had in mind to scare me with, but that's the picture I got. The name said it all.

No wonder he was mean; imagine going through life looking like that. I hoped my sympathy and understanding of his horrible handicap would work to my advantage, if he ever showed up. You can't defeat every monster with courage alone, especially those who are not bound by daylight or place.

VIII

WHERE IS MOM

I didn't hear Mom's call to breakfast one morning so I headed downstairs to see what was going on. Eating always won the battle with sleeping for me. Everyone but Mom was already at the table, nothing out of the ordinary there. Mom usually hovered between the table and the stove seeing to everyone else's needs. That morning she wasn't hovering. I wondered where she was and set off to investigate. I found her in the bathroom crying. As most children do, I went right in without knocking or permission. I was curious about the crying and shocked to see that she was going somewhere.

How did I know she was going somewhere? Easy, she was wearing her good dress. More accurately, she was wearing the best dress she had. I don't know how good it was, but she wore it almost every time she went off the farm. When she and Daddy went to town on occasional Saturdays, she wore that dress. When she visited kin folks, she wore that dress. It was also her going to the Christmas play at church dress, her visit the teacher at school dress, and her going to a funeral dress.

In our family and the community at large, your best attire was referred to as "Sunday-Go-To-Meet'n Clothes" and that's what Mom was wearing. It wasn't because she liked that dress so much; it was just that Mom chose to have only one good dress so my sisters and I could have more than one. If she was wearing it, she was going somewhere important.

Mom seldom left the farm. She was a working mom, but she didn't leave home to do it. She wasn't a *homemaker*; she was a HOME MAKER. Daddy made the living, Mommy made the home, and the two of them together managed to provide everything else our family needed to thrive, not just survive. It wasn't an easy life, but it was a good one. Mom's work took her many places, but off the farm wasn't one of them. She could always be found in or around our old Kentucky home in rural Lawrence County.

If she wasn't working in the house, there were lots of other places she might be. If Dad wasn't home, she might be at the barn feeding livestock and milking cows. In winter, she might be making a trip to the coal house for fueling the fireplaces and the Warm Morning stove. She made daily treks to the hen house to gather eggs and feed the chickens. And, she was often in the smoke house curing or cutting meat.

I thought the smoke house was a better place to get meat than the hen house. Hog butchering was gruesome, but it took on a festive quality with all the activities that surrounded the November event.

I stayed on the back porch until I heard the shots signaling the hogs were dead. Then in the company of someone else, I made my way up past the barn to the valley where giants might live just over the next hill. By the time I arrived, the pig had been bled and was on a wooden sled by the stream. A big black pot of water was boiling over an open fire to help scrap the hair off the hog. After that, the clean shaven animal was hung from a tree for butchering. I'll spare you the details.

Sounds disgusting doesn't it? It was, but since that work was handled by the men, it didn't seem that bad. What was unnatural was watching your Mom grab a chicken by the head and give it a full body twist, expertly breaking its' neck. Then she would stretch its' neck on the chopping block and decapitate the bird with one swift stroke of the hatchet.

The process of having chicken and dumplings for dinner got worse when the decapitated fowl started flopping all over the back yard. Blood was slung everywhere, and when the flopping stopped; the bird was dipped in boiling water so the feathers could be plucked.

The smell of boiling water on pig hair was aromatic compared to the smell of wet chicken feathers. And, we couldn't throw the feathers away. Oh no, *waste not, want not* was another family motto. We had to save them to make pillows.

Most parts of the chicken were edible, disgusting but edible. Daddy actually liked gizzards. I think the only part of a chicken Mom didn't use was the beak and guts. The smell of wet chicken feathers stayed in your nostrils until a big bowl of fluffy dumplings was placed on the dinner table.

The trauma of getting that meal together should have turned me into a vegetarian, but it didn't. I like all kinds of meat, and I especially like chicken. I can eat it baked or barbequed, in soup or stewed, and fried or fricasseed. I just don't like chickens. I can tolerate them in a hen house, laying eggs. I just don't like flopping headless chickens, mean flogging chickens, hysterically screeching chickens, or annoying clucking chickens. And, I especially do not like pecking, pooping chickens in the yard.

The other livestock stayed behind the gate. They ate there; they eliminated there. Nothing is worse than squishing chicken poop between your toes on a summer day. Stepping in chicken poop was worse than stepping on a honey bee. You might think there are worse things to step in on the farm, but you'd be wrong. Cow paddies can't surprise you; they're big enough to be seen from a distance. Chickens are the worst animals on the farm. It's not much of an insult to be called a cow paddy now is it?

Laundry was a weekly chore. When Mom was fix'n to put out a worsh'n, she was on the back porch filling tubs with water drawn from the well and filling the wringer Maytag with warm water carried from the kitchen. The process consisted of washing once in warm water, scrubbing stains on the worsh board, rinsing twice in cold water, then starching whatever needed to be starched.

Mom hung the wet clothes on the line to dry. The dried clothes were taken down, folded and put away. Those that were starched got sprinkled, rolled up, and ironed later. I hate ironing! Thankfully being the baby girl meant by the time I was big enough to iron, those big wavy crocheted doilies surrounding every lamp in the house were going out of style.

There was lots of seasonal work that had to be done too. Even with all the gardening that was necessary, spring was Mom's favorite time of year. She loved the sun and the results of her planting. The vegetable garden fed our bodies and the flower garden fed Mom's spirit. She didn't spend her spare time there because she didn't have spare time. But, she always found a way to make time for her flowers.

At the end of summer, Mom could be found over big kettles in the back yard preserving food. After the hogs were butchered in November, Mom rendered lard in those same pots. She had a host of chores, but most of her time was spent with food. She was either planting it, weeding it, gathering it, slaughtering it, preserving it or cooking it.

We began each day with a hot meal and ended the day with a hot supper. When we weren't in school, a hot dinner (lunch) was added to the day's chores, especially if men folk were working in the fields. Breakfast was usually homemade biscuits, gravy, eggs, and meat.

On the particular morning I'm recalling, a hot breakfast was already on the table, even though Mom was upset and apparently going somewhere. Where was she going and why was she crying? Inquiring minds wanted to know.

I had school that day. I had questions. I needed answers. Most importantly, what was I doing for lunch? Would Mom be there when I got home? Who was fixing supper? Things needed to be settled. She couldn't just put on her good dress and go somewhere early in the morning, on a weekday!

Unless...there must have been another tragedy.

IX

THE TRAGEDY

The only other time I had experienced that type of wakeup call was when I was about five years old. Mom was crying that morning too. Even Daddy seemed upset. There had been a radio news report about a school bus accident. I remember feeling kind of shaky inside as I listened to the conversation taking place between Mom, Dad and Granny.

I heard the words **wrecked, river,** and **drowned**. Then the phrase, "searching for survivors". I couldn't even form words to ask if my brother and sister would be coming home. My two oldest brothers were already gone. They were in the Army and the Air Force, but they still came home sometimes. I knew the adults were talking about children who wouldn't be coming home. If something bad happened to them, who would make me a sling shot or stand between me and the horse? Who would provide petticoats and high heels for playing dress up with my friend? That might have been the only time in my young life that I was too upset to eat.

I learned the tragedy had occurred in Floyd County. That's where we used to live and where many of my relatives still lived: grandpa, uncles, aunts, and dozens of cousins. Mom had one sister and nine brothers, so when I say dozens of cousins, I mean that literally. Several of them rode that bus to school in Prestonsburg. Mom and Dad were getting ready to go there. With the memory of that morning in my mind, I assumed another tragedy had occurred.

I was surprised to learn it wasn't another tragedy; Mom was just going to the doctor. Going to the doctor! Are you kidding me? That was no reason to cry. Crying wasn't allowed in our family. Well, I might be overstating a bit; let's just say crying was highly discouraged. We didn't cry when we were scared. We didn't cry when we were hurt. We didn't cry when we were sick. We didn't even cry when we got shots.

There were some crybabies at school who started as soon as the vaccination nurse showed up, but not us. Why would someone in our family cry about going to the doctor? The only time we were allowed to cry was when we got a whoop'n. Then we better cry or our parents would give us something to cry about.

I got my fair share. Mom's punishment was usually issued with hand or switch. Nothing says discipline like a stinging peach tree switch. Adding insult to injury, I often had to pull it off the tree myself. You bet I cried; those things could really get a grip on bare legs.

Playing with two childhood friends, a brother and sister, I was amazed at what I witnessed when their two younger sisters got a whoop'n. They were misbehaving and when their mom said, "That's it girls, I'm getting the belt." They started crying immediately and begged her not to use the RED BELT. I had never heard such wailing after a spanking let alone before the first lick fell.

I asked what was so terrible about the RED BELT. They said it was from their mom's Sunday Go To Meet'n dress. She spanked them with it after church one day and it barely hurt. Since then, they had perfected their act to insure the RED BELT was their mom's 'go to' for punishment. My folks weren't that gullible.

Daddy didn't whip often; he didn't need to. We were obedient. Actually, Perfection and Good as Gold were obedient. I tended to push the boundaries every now and then. Good as Gold never got spanked by Daddy; I remember getting three. Daddy didn't seem to object to my pushing the boundaries as long as I didn't cross them.

My first spanking was for deliberately hurting Little Brother. The second was for giving Mom grief. It came one Sunday when we had company for dinner, which was almost every Sunday. The custom was for men to eat in the dining room. The children ate on the porch standing with their plates on the rail. Women hovered around waiting on the men and children, and then sat down for a somewhat uninterrupted meal in the kitchen.

I decided I wanted to eat at the dining room table instead of on the porch. Mom told me no and went on with her last minute dinner preparations. She simply ignored my continued whining request, so I laid down across the threshold between the kitchen and dining room. That's where Daddy found me having a little tantrum when he and the other men came in for dinner. That maneuver really paid off; I got to eat at the dining room table! I just hadn't planned on doing it alone, on a stinging bottom, after everyone else had eaten.

It helped me realize that getting what I asked for, was not always a good thing. Seeking your father's will is usually the best policy. Seeking The Father's will is always the best policy.

> Therefore do not be unwise, but understand
> what the will of the Lord is.
> **Ephesians 5:17 (NKJV)**

My third and final spanking came when I was about seven. Dad was building something at the barn and I was in the saddle house playing with sacks of shiny nails. I was wearing purple pedal pushers with pockets. I put some of the nails in my pocket so I could ask Big Brother to make something for me, probably a slingshot.

When Dad finished working and was putting tools away he asked if I had anymore nails. I said no and we started back to the house. About halfway down the lane, I started to run and the nails began jingle. Busted!

"I want you to understand something," Dad said. "I'm not spanking you for taking the nails. I'm spanking you because you lied." He was not saying stealing was okay. That one whoop'n reinforced two commandments and one certainty. Thou shalt not steal, thou shalt not lie, and thou certainly shalt not lie about stealing. Every time I got whipped by Dad, it was definitely something to cry about.

There's a cute little saying much over used these days, *put on your big girl pants and get over it*. I think that saying might have originated in my family. Not my immediate family, but ancestors who arrived many years ago on a boat from Germany.

I assume my great, great grandfather, who came to fight in the in the American Revolution, was not a crybaby. There might have been crybabies at Valley Forge, but I'd bet the farm my ancestor wasn't one of them. If you're smiling now, you are either of German descent, or well acquainted with that demonstrative, sympathetic people group.

Let me explain to those who may not be familiar with the German psyche. When Fuzzy, the family cat had kittens, one was sick and probably going to die. *Mein grandpa* picked up his cane and with one swift hit to the head, killed the little kitten. It was a mercy killing; the kitten was suffering. You can't witness something like that without learning not to be a cry baby, **especially** when you're sick. And yet, Mom was crying about going to the doctor even though the kitten killer was *her* dad!

Grandpa was rough on crybabies. Did Mom not care if her dad thought she was weak? Their relationship sure was different than mine and Daddy's. I couldn't understand what was going on with her; the excuse didn't make sense. She said the doctor was just going to confirm she had something called Sugar Diabetes.

How did she know that? She had consulted the family medical book of course. It was a big, red, well used tome of diseases, symptoms, and treatments. That book served as our family's equivalent of an emergency room, Care Now and Doc in a Box. Rural Kentuckians only went to the doctor for serious stuff. Everything else was treated with castor oil, turpentine, Epsom salt and iodine. Folks took care of injuries and sicknesses at home. That's mostly because they were too busy, too poor, or too far away to get professional help.

The rule of thumb for going to the doctor was losing a body part bigger than a thumb. Even if it was barely hanging on; one of the remedies mentioned above usually worked. The dangling part was tied back on with strips of worn out bed sheets. My little brother's big toe was hanging on just by the skin, not once, but twice when he was a little. He was doctored at home and still has that little piggy that went to market.

Doctored and *doctor'n* are verbs in Hillbilly speak. To clear things up, the medical doctrine for country folk was to do the doctor'n at home. Some injuries required resting a *spell* (a period of time). It could be as short as the time it took to tie a rag around an injury or as long as it takes for a broken bone to knit back together.

Some words we used stay archived until the family gets together. Then we fully growed young'uns throw them around and try to figure out how they originated. *Fully growed* means any mature human, plant, or animal and *young'uns* is obviously those not yet fully growed. One word we had trouble with was *kyarn*. We were discussing it one day in our uncle's presence. He told us it was a handed down mispronunciation of the word carrion, meaning rotting flesh. That made perfect sense because we used that word to describe anything that smelled really horrible.

Many words had dual and even triple meanings. A spell wasn't just a length of time. It could also refer to something a witch might cast. A *kiver* could be used on a bed or a container. Extra kiver was needed on cold nights. A mess of greens was kivered when they started to bile. *Bile* is boil, but it could be green liquid coming out of your mouth when everything else has been thrown up.

A *mess* could be the bile you're throwing up, an amount of food, or muddy snow tracked in the house. Mom could often be heard lamenting, "Mess and gom, mess and gom! Why are you young'uns always messing and gomming?" We had no idea where the word gom came from; it described sticky stuff. The top of the honey jar was usually gommed up because we wouldn't clean the rim after pouring honey.

The word *piece* could mean a section of quilt, a portion of food, or distance. A 'right smart little piece' down the road meant you should probably drive instead of walk. Close neighbors lived just a little piece down or a little piece up the road. Other communities were a right smart little piece away. We also assigned prepositions to community names and locations.

Some folks lived *up* Horse Picture or *up on* Young Branch. You had to go *up on* Young Branch before you could *go over on* Lost Creek or *around on* Hatfield. Some neighbors lived *down on* Nelson or *over on* Wiley Branch. The school bus picked up *round on* Charley before picking up the children who lived on George's Creek.

Round on Charley really confused me. I don't know how old I was, but older than I should have been, before discovering the lyrics 'Round yon Virgin' of Silent Night, did not refer to where Mary and baby Jesus lived.

Those preposition assignments might have had something to do with George's Creek. It flowed south to north through our community, before making its' way to the Ohio River. I think it was a tributary of the Big Sandy River, but I'm not sure.

Going down south and heading up north makes sense; not in our community. We went up to Paintsville which was south, up the creek. We went down to Louisa which was north, down the creek. I'm only speculating, but it could have developed from barge traffic moving goods up and down the river in the old days.

Is it any wonder I have no sense of direction? Maybe I shouldn't put all the blame on the flow of the creek, but several of us George's Creek girls got lost in our own community for an entire day. To be fair, it was a creek bed that eventually came to our rescue.

On a whim one Saturday morning, we headed off to visit Table Rock, a big, round, flat topped boulder in the hills. We found the rock and a few of us made it to the top. That feat required climbing a tall tree next to the rock, getting far enough out on a branch that would bend, then dropping on to the top. Getting off was harder; it required grabbing the limb from a running jump so you could shiny back down to the ground.

Feeling proud of conquering a 'boy' challenge, we headed off to find Upstairs/Downstairs Cave, another rock quest. I don't know why the other girls went, but the sun was shining, I wasn't alone and being almost invincible, I went.

Looking back, we really should have told someone where we were going. Telling the boys we got to the top of Table Rock AND in the upstairs of Upstairs/Downstairs Cave was too alluring. We couldn't risk our parents telling us we couldn't go. Besides, one of the girls had some sort of idea where it was. She had been there once with her brother.

We were full of anticipation and adventure the first hour. We were unenthusiastic, but hopeful, the next hour. That was quickly followed with thirst, poison oak, and fear. The sun was still shining so I was okay, but some of the younger girls started crying. We continued our disoriented wandering for another hour or so.

The sun was going down and my panic going up. We were lost and our parents didn't even know we were gone. Granny wasn't going to be much help with this. One of the girls tried to use the sun as a guide, but none of us had a clue what direction to take.

We ran into a dry creek bed and one of the girls had enough common sense to suggest following it down the mountain. The sun was almost gone before we came out into a garden area. There was a man leaving his outhouse and we asked him for directions. We were a right smart little piece away from where we all lived. Our adventure began up Horse Picture and ended down on Nelson. Adding insult to injury, no one even knew we were missing.

I hope you enjoyed that detour. Now, back to Mom. She was going to the doctor because she thought she had a disease called Sugar Diabetes. I figured it must be something bad because of Mom's crying, but I couldn't understand how anything involving sugar could be bad?

Sugar was good! It's what made desserts yummy. Mom used it in homemade ice cream and snow cream. She used it in and sprinkled it on fresh baked cookies. Three whole cups went into her homemade chocolate candy. She used sugar to make cobblers, pies, and cakes. Even occasional birthday cakes for one of us, had crunchy letters spelling 'HAPPY BIRTHDAY' made from sugar.

I loved sugar! I ate spoons full when no one was looking. How could Mom get something bad from something so good? Wait...come to think of it, I had been warned about eating too much sugar. Now what was it? They did tell me something bad could happen if I ate too much. Even Granny said something the last time she caught me eating pure sugar from the sugar bowl. If I could only remember… Wait, it's coming to me…Oh No, MOM HAS WORMS!

DIARY OF A DIABETIC

X

THE SYNDROME

You should know that at an early age, I was already developing SOP Syndrome. I'm not sure how rare it is; no clinical studies have been done. Not many people outside my immediate family have heard of it. The only reason they have is because I invented it and named it. SOPS is an acronym for **S**carlett **O**'Hara/**P**ollyanna **S**yndrome.

It's my coping mechanism for dealing with life. It's really more of an attitude than a syndrome, but SOPS seemed more accurate than SOPA. Here's how it works. Like Scarlett in *Gone with the Wind*, when faced with a difficulty I couldn't cope with, I said, "I'll just worry about that later." And when things went wrong, as things often do, my Pollyanna attitude carried me through.

On that particular day with Mom crying, her going to the doctor, and the sugar slander I was hearing, my SOPS kicked in. All I needed to know was: will Mom be back and when will Mom be back? All I needed to hear was yes and today. After receiving those very answers, I headed to the breakfast table to eat. And that was my introduction to diabetes.

Mom and the big red medical book were right, she had diabetes. I was glad to find out no worms were involved and that's all I really needed to know. Nothing changed in my world because of her diabetes. I didn't learn anything about the disease for a long, long time.

As the years passed, I gained knowledge about the disease and *knew* because of family history, all of Mom's children had an increased risk of developing diabetes. I also *knew* that maintaining a healthy body weight and an active life style could decrease that risk factor.

I use the word *knew* instead of learned because I have discovered that people can gain all sorts of knowledge without learning a thing. That's how it was for me and diabetes. I had secondhand knowledge through Mom's struggles, then firsthand knowledge from my own. But unfortunately, I never learned much.

It took decades of learning the hard way from all the knowledge I had. I'm not sure it's possible to learn the easy way. Think about babies. Most, not all, but most are born with the ability to cry, eat, and poop. They don't learn how to do it; that knowledge was programmed into them by God. Everything after that is learned the hard way. You *know* not to touch a flame, but only learn not to touch it after getting burned. As far as my diabetes was concerned, I just kept playing in the fire.

I have discovered that the amount of time it takes to learn something, usually depends on the person being taught. Some people learn to play the piano after years of half-hearted practice and parent enforced lessons. A few are programmed to play by ear and practice on their own. Others learn quickly from lots of practice and from applying what they *know*. But all three types of pianists hit wrong notes along the way.

My drawn-out learning curve for diabetes was in part due to my Scarlett O'Hara/Pollyanna Syndrome. The syndrome itself was not a bad thing. It got me through, and continues to get me through when things go wrong, **as things often do**. But in respect to diabetes, it allowed me to abdicate my responsibility. I decided diabetes was an old person's disease that I would 'just worry about later." Later came, but it took years. And when I finally got the diagnosis, the years seemed like the blink of an eye.

Time passed; I grew up. Along the way I graduated from high school, graduated from business school, worked in Kentucky, worked in Ohio, came back to Kentucky then went Texas, all before my twenty-first birthday.

Texas happened because I took advantage of an opportunity to visit my oldest brother who lived there. The visit turned into a job offer, the job turned into finding Mr. Right. Mr. Right turned into my husband and Texas became my home. My adult life truly began in Texas.

I grew up quickly when Daddy died of an unexpected heart attack just three months after I got married. SOPS wasn't much help then. I eventually had to put on my big girl pants and face it, because getting over it wasn't easy.

I had a wonderful husband, home, and career. Then I had the blessing of children. Life was good. The years kept passing. Mom's diabetes went from diet control, to oral meds, to insulin injections. I knew a lot about the disease; the only thing I learned was how to give Mom shots. She taught me so I could give them in her hip or arm. That gave her thighs a rest, otherwise she had to give herself daily injections.

My husband and I were married for three years when we discovered the odds of us having children were extremely slim to none. Now, just where did I put those big girl pants? We were told there was a drug that might improve our chances, but after careful consideration, we decided to leave it in God's hands. I figured He knew I wasn't really mother material. And to be honest, I never really felt that overwhelming desire for motherhood like so many women do.

Pulling up those big girl pants wasn't that difficult for me. It was harder on my husband because he really wanted children. Since that probably wasn't going to happen, we became a DINK couple, duel income no kids. Our third bedroom became a den and our backyard an oasis of pool and hot tub. We concentrated on careers, drove German imports and became upwardly mobile. We were foot loose and fancy free for nine years.

Our life outside work revolved around a social organization I belonged to. During one of the events, a sorority sister offered me something to eat. I declined with a, "No thanks, everything is giving me indigestion lately." She jokingly said, "Maybe you're pregnant. That's what happened to my sister with both of her pregnancies." We laughed at the impossibility then she said, "Stranger things have happened. You're not late are you?" Me? No way, every twenty nine days like clockwork. Let's see, I'm due TWO WEEKS AGO! So much for the odds, I was pregnant!

Everyone was thrilled for us; we were giddy with excitement and anticipation. All too soon, devastation arrived when I miscarried at twelve weeks. We couldn't wrap our mind around what had happened. Sadness and anger vied for control of my emotions. There were many dark days. Why? There was guilt. Was it my fault? Did I do something wrong? Did I fail to do something right?

Pollyanna started helping me focus on the positive. If it happened once, it could happen again. I was able to at least be thankful for the experience of being pregnant. In that short time, I discovered a depth of love I didn't know existed. I also discovered that material 'things' have very little value.

Do not lay up for yourself treasure on earth, where moth
and rust destroy and where thieves break in and steal;
Matthew 6:19 (NKJV)

One night a cousin and close friend called to check on me. I was trying to explain the blessings from the experience when he said, 'Blessings?" I continued to explain and when I finished he said, "That's just so like you. You're the only person I know who digs through a pile of horse manure until they find a pony." When I stopped laughing, I knew I would recover. Laughter is the best medicine and it can bring healing. If you can laugh, joy is not far away.

A life filled with humor is a good life and sometimes it's the best way to survive. I know there's a time for every purpose under heaven and I can be serious for short periods of time, when absolutely necessary. But, there are just so many times when humor can get a job done quicker than anything else. I've been accused of being irreverent because I have the knack of finding humor in unexpected places.

Visiting the city of a sorority sister, our group of four were stopped at an intersection when Hometown Sis started telling us a local story. That particular intersection was where the back door of an ambulance popped open sending patient and gurney rolling down the street. The more she elaborated about the tragic accident, the funnier and more unbelievable it got. Two of us eventually burst into hysterical laughter. The other two, indignant and not amused sisters thought we were horrible. Their outrage and chastising only made us laugh harder.

I do seem to find humor in odd places. When I went to visit a friend who had been hospitalized for a psychological disorder, I had no idea what to say. So when I walked through the door, the first thing that popped out of my mouth was, "What in the world were thinking; **have you lost your mind**?" Without missing a beat, my friend said, "So they tell me." We just looked at each other and started laughing. The barriers were down, the awkwardness gone, and we were able to talk like old friends should.

An example of my misunderstood sense of humor occurred at choir practice one Wednesday night. A somber announcement was made that a longtime and much loved local pastor had died. Proper comments of sorrow were being expressed and someone asked what happened. We learned he had died while in the pulpit preaching. "Wow, what a way to go," I blurted out. Shocked faces turned toward me. In the dead (no pun intended) silence, I saw a pair of twinkling eyes instead of judging eyes. They belonged to a cute little blond alto who sat in my section.

When rehearsal was finally over, I beat a quick retreat thinking choir might not be my place of service. Then Blond Alto walked up and said, "I know exactly what you mean. You weren't being flippant, you just meant getting called to heaven preaching The Word *was* a great way to go." At least one person in choir understood me.

God has a great sense of humor. There are examples of it throughout the Bible. I've never understood how anyone with the joy of the Lord in their heart can keep it from showing on their face.

> A merry heart makes a cheerful countenance,
> But by sorrow of the heart the spirit is broken.
> **Proverbs 15:13 (NKJV)**

My joy waned for a while after losing the baby. But, I found hope in focusing on the blessings. Miraculously, one year later our first son was born. You see, God doesn't deal in odds; He simply says yes, no, or not now. When I found the courage and faith to ask for a child, he said yes immediately. But even with that kind of miracle staring me in the face, my faith waivered. I had a miracle, but wondered why God granted it? Why would He put something as precious as a baby in my care? Surly He knew I wasn't mother material.

Motherhood is a physical **and** an emotional eruption. I had no concept of how much my parents loved me until I became a parent. I was completely overwhelmed by the realization of how much God loved me. I had absolutely NO IDEA that kind of love was even possible.

I never looked at Christmas and especially Easter the same way again. I could not fathom Mary's pain when her son was nailed to a cross. I knew all things were possible with God, but how could He send His son to die for me?

Understanding was slow in coming and I had many questions ranging from deep mysteries to the everyday ridiculous. Why did I lose the first baby? Why did I get the second miracle? Why was my mom going home instead of staying to help me raise my son? Didn't she care about her grandson? She knew I was inadequate. Hadn't she and Mother-in-Law spent the last two weeks reinforcing that fact?

The night before she left, I remember lying awake thinking, how could she leave me with this precious baby. Thankfully, exhaustion and Mom took over and I got a good night's sleep for the first time in two weeks, and the last time for 12 months. The next morning, I said a confident goodbye to Mother and spent a great first day alone with my son. The rest of the year was spent in and out of my big girl pants.

Some days were absolute bliss when I was the picture of motherhood. Some days, I kissed Husband goodbye in the morning and glared him home in the afternoon, still wearing the same gown I slept in the night before. I was jealous of his escape. Nothing seemed to change much for him. He got up, had the luxury of taking a shower, got dressed, went to work, ate lunch and had conversations with adults. EVERYTHING in me and in my world had been turned inside out.

My love for the Little Prince was overwhelming. I marveled at the blessing and miracle of having him. But, just trying to cope when things were good was difficult. When he was sick or cranky, I barely had the energy to feed him and change his diaper. There were a few really bad days when the constant whining and crying got so bad, my husband would come home from work and give our happy, healthy son a break from his whining, crying, mother; I was the one out of control.

Baby Blues, really? That term sounds like you might be a little bit sad; that's not what I had. I didn't know it at the time, but I had Post-partum depression. Some days were wonderful! Some were hopeless! Expectant parents need more information about dealing with those times. I only realized what I had with our first son, when I didn't experience it with the second one.

When Little Prince was nine months old, I was pregnant again. Unfortunately, another miscarriage only added to the emotional mess that was me. I was sad and joyous. I felt blessed and cursed. I was guilty and angry. What was wrong with me? I had enough faith to ask God for a miracle, one He granted. I just hadn't grown enough in faith to ask for His strength and guidance.

Be anxious for nothing, but in everything by prayer and supplication, with thanksgiving, let your requests be made known to God; and the peace of God, which surpasses all understanding, will guard your hearts and minds through Jesus Christ.
Philippians 4:6&7 (NKJV)

I didn't know how to trust God and I had too much pride to ask anyone for help. I wasn't in control, but I couldn't relinquish control to someone else without looking weak. I thought if my mother managed to raise seven happy, (almost) well-adjusted children, why was dealing with one so difficult for me? I needed to figure that out, because getting pregnant didn't seem to be a problem any longer.

I eventually found my mind which had been missing in action, and I regained some control of my emotions and life. My husband and I started thinking about having another child. We talked to every 'only child' we came in contact with; all but one said they wished they weren't an only. Three and a half years after the Little Prince was born, we had Sweetest Heart. And three years after that, The Baby was born.

XI

BIRTHING BABIES

I spent most of my thirties pregnant. There had been some issues with the pregnancies, especially with the first two deliveries. I wasn't good breeding stock, not broad enough in the hips to deliver easily. It took twenty-eight hours of labor before our first son was born.

I had been on bed rest the last month and a fetal stress test hastened his arrival. We reported to the hospital at five on a Thursday morning. After twelve hours of induced labor, we were given the option of having a C-section or restarting the drug again the next morning, if he had not arrived by that time.

Thinking this would be our only child and wanting to experience the beauty of natural childbirth, we decided against a C-section. After all, we were the valedictorian and salutatorian of our childbirth classes. We were prepared; we were ready. I had been the ideal student and now I was the ideal patient. I could have been the poster girl for natural childbirth...THE FIRST TWELVE HOURS!

Sometimes I think a LOT higher of myself than I ought. I certainly ought not to have when it came to childbirth. I was sure it couldn't be that bad. I assumed all the horror stories I had heard were exaggerations or from the lips of big crybabies. If childbirth was that bad, no one would have a second child, right?

I had lots of faults; being a wimp wasn't one of them. I was told the drug to induce would make labor pains worse, ABSOLUTELY CORRECT. However, I was also told it would shorten the duration of the labor. REALLY? I figured I could handle anything for a short period of time. That theory might have held up if, the length of the labor had **actually been shorter.**

When given the option of a C-section after going through **twelve hours of HARD labor,** I listened. And, it wasn't easy to hear with all the moaning and writhing I was doing. My husband couldn't be in the operating room for an unscheduled section. We figured labor couldn't possibly be much longer, so we opted to wait. My husband really wanted to witness the birth.

My 'should have been a doctor instead of an engineer' husband thought the birth of our sons was the greatest thing he had ever witnessed. I can't argue that point because I never got to witness the birth of either one of them. With the first two deliveries, I was focused on the survival of me and the baby instead of the mirror reflecting the birth. He even witnessed the section delivery with our third son; I was unconscious.

After that delivery, I threatened to have security remove him and a friend from my room. She wanted details and my husband was more than happy to oblige. I didn't need or want to hear about being cut open or how my fat layer looked. He described my uterus like a football and our third son like an alien poking his head out of my stomach. It was amusing, but it was just too painful for me to laugh. Stitches!

I was glad he got to see it, but if I had wanted to know what my insides looked like, I would have chosen to be awake for the delivery. I fluctuated about it for a bit, but decided I was okay with finding out the sex of the baby when I regained consciousness. I came to with my husband saying, "Wake up, we have another beautiful boy."

I eventually had to tell him to go to medical school and stop offering to be the delivery coach for every pregnant woman we knew. He volunteered every time an expectant dad said he did not want to be in the delivery room. He was scaring expectant couples and starting to worry me.

My point, his witnessing the birth played a major role in our decision to pass on the C-section. As for thinking it couldn't take much longer, SO WRONG! I had natural labor pains every ten minutes the remainder of the night. At six THE NEXT MORNING, the drip resumed and our son did not make an appearance until shortly before ten Friday morning.

> To the woman he said: "I will greatly multiply your sorrow and conception; In pain you shall bring forth children; Your desire shall be for your husband, And he shall rule over you."
> **Genesis 3:16 (NKJV)**

Pandemonium broke out in the delivery room. The Little Prince got wedged so tightly in the birth canal they thought a broken collar bone would result. For that reason, I wasn't surprised or scared when the same thing happened with our second son. They didn't even strap my legs in the stirrups for his birth. If there was a repeat performance, my body would be twisted and contorted to aid in the delivery.

It was a repeat performance, but since the Little Prince did not suffer a broken collar bone, I thought Sweetest Heart would be okay too. They mentioned possible nerve damage to his arm, but I didn't give it much thought. He was here and healthy! I started concentrating on successful breast feeding.

I tell you these childbirth stories because…Well duh, WOMEN LOVE TO SHARE THEIR CHILDBIRTH STORIES! I call my sons every year on their birthdays just to say, "Do you want to hear about the day (days in the Little Prince's case) you were born?" All three of them say, "No Mom really, I'm good. I've got it. You suffered."

I also share so you can understand why breast feeding was so important to me. I failed miserably the first time. I believe one reason was because the hospital gave him a bottle, even though I told them I would be breast feeding.

Nursing for the first time after an uneventful birth would be stressful. Doing it after a marathon labor, a traumatic delivery and a triple episiotomy, with a baby who had already been nursed from a bottle was anything but natural and successful.

I might have overcome those issues if not for the expert tutelage I received from Mother and Mother-in-Law. Mom's opinion was that my milk was too weak and the production too little to meet his nutritional needs. AND, she thought my breasts were too big for him to breathe easily while nursing.

She could have been right about the milk. I was in a lot of pain for several days and was experiencing rapid weight loss. But, thinking my breasts were 'too big' to nurse! This from a woman who nursed seven babies and wore a bra with a six hook closure in the back. The only difference in the size of our breasts was their inflation level. Hers were huge and flat; mine were huge and inflated.

Adding to the situation, Mother-in-Law was sharing her opinion with anyone who would listen: friends, neighbors, relatives, strangers, florist delivery drivers, etc. She took great pains to explain that the breast feeding just wasn't going well. Tsk, tsk, shake of the head, knowing look. "The baby is rejecting her; he can sense her inexperience and tension. If she would only learn to hold him properly, things would improve."

One day the moms had me propped up on some pillows for another go at breast feeding when my husband appeared in the doorway to check on OUR progress. I'll never forget the look on his face when he saw me propped up on the bed with my breast sticking through the slit of my nursing gown. My arms were at my sides useless. I was pretty sure I had entered the *Twilight Zone* and was listening for Rod Serling's voice.

My husband wasn't shocked at my big inflated, exposed breast. He had already seen way more of me in the delivery room than a husband should see. What stunned him was seeing his mother holding our son to my breast, while my mother pressed and manipulated my breast so the baby could breathe easier.

My response to his unspoken question, "What in the world is going on in here?" was "If my breast wasn't attached, they wouldn't need me at all." Do you have some insight as to why I wasn't getting the hang (pardon the pun) of breast feeding?

I was determined to get it right with the second baby, I alerted everyone on staff that I **was** breast feeding. They obliged and brought him to me in the recovery room. When I put him to my now more enormous breast (I didn't know they made F cups), everything worked the way it was designed to work. I was nursing that little sweetheart all alone and without expert advice or help. My breasts were being used as intended instead of getting unwanted attention.

I was euphoric over being able to nurse. I knew he was receiving pain medication and they were keeping him in disposable shirts so they didn't have to move his arm much, but that was the extent off my knowledge regarding his arm. I learned about it when I was getting him dressed to go home from the hospital.

I tore his paper shirt off and noticed ink on his curled up fist. I thought it must have gotten there when they did his footprints. Maybe they take hand prints too. I couldn't remember. I reached for a wipe and started for his hand when the nurse said, "Be careful mom, his arm is still tender." I took another look. It wasn't ink, it was bruising.

Only then did I notice he was not moving his left arm. His legs kicked and his right arm was moving, but not his left. It was curled up close to his body. The nurse said it was probably only temporary damage, but I started bawling. He was in pain and couldn't move his arm while I was using mine to pat myself on the back for breast feeding. Fortunately there wasn't any permanent damage to his arm. Unfortunately there wasn't any damage to my SOP Syndrome either.

XII

GESTATIONAL DIABETES

By the time we were expecting our third and final child, I was considered high risk from all the issues with past pregnancies. I'm sure my age and the amount of weight I gained with Sweetest Heart factored into the high risk equation.

I gained fifteen pounds with our first son and lost it before coming home from the hospital. Another fifteen melted away during the next three weeks. Suffice it to say getting The Little Prince here was not easy. After a second miscarriage nine months later, the weight started returning. I was twenty pounds shy of an all-time high when Sweetest Heart was conceived and I gained almost forty during that pregnancy. I wasn't great with child; I was enormous!

The Dallas Cowboys were playing football the Sunday he was born. That attentive childbirth coach of mine was watching the game in **my** labor room. **We** were having a baby, but I was the one laboring. I remember hearing the announcer giving stats for one of the linemen and thinking, Good Grief, I weigh the same as he does, and he's a foot taller!

I'm sure my weight, age, previous miscarriages, toxemia and a traumatic delivery were causes for concern. And sure enough, a traumatic delivery did occur a second time. However, glucose levels was not a concern with the first two births.

When The Baby was on the way, the doctor said expectant mothers were now being tested for gestational diabetes. I was familiar with Type I and Type II, but had never heard of gestational diabetes. The doctor explained the condition and said it just required taking a simple blood test.

The nurse gave instructions to arrive at the lab by 9:30 the next morning. I couldn't eat or drink anything before the tests because they would be monitoring my fasting blood sugar levels. "Did you say test-s, as in plural? I thought the doctor said test, singular." The *simple test* boiled down to this: drink some sweet stuff on an empty stomach, hang around the lab and get blood drawn every fifteen minutes. Like the doctor said, *simple*.

I showed up that morning a bit queasy. Not much of a mystery there since I was pregnant and fasting! I signed in and Lab Coat came out. He handed me *not some*, but half a gallon of a sweet syrupy mixture to drink. Guess what I discovered?

SUGAR DOESN'T ALWAYS TASTE GOOD

AND

SIMPLE DOES'T ALWAYS MEAN EASY

Lab Coat went on to caution me not to throw up or we would have to start the test over. Oh yes he did, in a tone suggesting how inconvenient that would be for him.

I guess he thought most of us stay at home pregnant women were a pampered lot and without the caution, we might waste the time of those who actually had to work for a living. I had just rolled out of bed myself four hours earlier and was wondering how I would manage to fill the remainder of my leisurely day.

It wouldn't be considerate to waste the professional's time retaking the test, so maybe I'd take in a movie, have lunch with the girls or do some shopping. I was well rested. I was only up twice going to the bathroom and just once with Sweetest Heart. He started talking in his sleep about needing a show and tell item for school. I had lengthy sleep conversations with him quite often.

That morning I made coffee and watched my husband enjoy it because I was fasting. When he went to work, I could have gotten another three to five minutes of sleep. Instead, I laid out meat for supper and clothes for the boys, got the *Show and Tell* item for my nocturnal mumbling boy, signed a permission slip, packed a lunch and loaded backpacks.

I started the washer, took a shower, woke the boys, fixed their breakfast, got us dressed and in the car. I picked up car pool kid, dropped him and eldest at elementary school, took youngest and *Show and Tell* to pre-school, then headed to the lab across town.

I totally understood how difficult it would have been for Lab Coat to open another bottle and hand it to me. I was the one who got to relax and have a syrup cocktail. The only thing keeping the process from being a mini vacation was having a little umbrella in my drink.

I guess the hormones were making me think more highly of myself than I ought. But once I understood how much work was involved for Lab Coat, I was on board with doing whatever made his job easier. I would have plenty of time for me. I had two whole hours before I had to pick up Sweetest Heart from pre-school. Sometimes I just don't think of others first.

I was surprised to learn that throwing up was something that could be controlled. I wondered just how many times someone doesn't throw up because they were **cautioned** not to. It never worked with Sweetest Heart. The words 'me tick' struck fear in our hearts.

We could caution all we wanted, but those words meant we had ten to fifteen seconds to reach the bathroom, a bag or a bucket. Sometimes we only made it as far as the lobby of a restaurant before the throwing up began. I just assumed that if throwing up **was** an option, no one **would opt** to do it? But once again, I was wrong!

The blood testing wasn't a big deal; pregnant women are accustomed to being nauseous and uncomfortable. The BIG DEAL was keeping the sweet stuff down on an empty stomach. After one taste, I was sure I couldn't keep it down but I was committed to keeping it down. There was no way I could drink it twice in one day. It would be in everyone's best interest if I did not have to come back another day. I learned a great lesson in control from that test. Sometimes throwing up **is** an option.

I was one of the first few who tested positive for gestational diabetes. My OB sent me to a specialist to manage the condition. You would think after all these years some physician would have perfected the treatment, but it was still the practice of medicine. And for women who had gestational diabetes, the practice was just beginning.

My OB said I most likely had the same condition with the other pregnancies. Birth weight was a good indicator and I delivered big. Little Prince weighed almost 9 pounds and Sweetest Heart almost 10. When number three was on the way, a C-section was scheduled. The doctor said delivering another linebacker vaginally was too risky, and we were both getting too old for all that delivery room drama.

The specialist I saw was my first experience with a woman doctor. I thought she would have a better perspective of a woman's body and be more sympathetic and compassionate about women's health issues. At my first appointment she gave me a list of requirements that would be necessary if I wanted to avoid my baby's death. Did she really think it was necessary to use the word IF? So much for compassion and understanding.

I wish it had been just a bad first impression which was later over-shadowed by personality and bedside manner. Most of all, I'd like to say her gestational diabetes experience made up for all her other shortcomings. Unfortunately I can't. I never discovered a personality and since she never bothered to check on our bedside…

Being raised under the 'put on your big girl pants' philosophy, I didn't need hand holding. My OB wasn't a compassionate man. He was blunt, but I liked his cutting wit and quick sense of humor. Like I said, humor can heal. I didn't need his compassion; I needed his expertise. And, it certainly helped that he found joy in his work.

> So I perceived that nothing is better than that a man should
> rejoice in his own works, for that is his heritage. For who
> can bring him to see what will happen after him?
> **Ecclesiastes 3:22 (NKJV)**

I was on bedrest the last month of my pregnancy with the Little Prince. OB told me to start taking it easy at the seven month checkup. Unfortunately, my SOP Syndrome said I could wait until after the Founder's Day Banquet for my sorority. At the next checkup, my blood pressure and urine protein levels were elevated and he wanted to know if I had been taking it easy. "Not yet," I said and started to make excuses. He gave me the 'don't be stupid' look and said, "Things could get serious very quickly."

I asked how I could be so sick and feel so good. He said, "Would it be easier if you were hemorrhaging?" Not compassionately, he reminded me I felt great before the miscarriage started too. It was harsh but warranted. Still, in comparison to the Specialist, my OB was kindly Dr. Welby and compassionate Dr. Kildare all rolled into one.

Here's how I remember the basic consultation with the Specialist: give yourself two shots of insulin in the stomach each day, prick your finger seven times a day to monitor glucose levels, keep a journal of those glucose levels, follow this strict diet, and keep a log of everything you eat.

"Did you say two shots a day?" Yes, and I will be admitting you to the hospital tomorrow to learn how to do it. You'll be there three days taking classes and being monitored. Shocked, I asked, "Is there another option?" She answered with a question, "Do you want a healthy baby?" Then she said come back in two weeks.

OK, I was going to the hospital. No problem, maybe my six year old could take care of the three year old. I'll spare you the details and just say, my husband was truly Mr. Wonderful. He took care of everything and even made sure I had a private room to get some rest; I did the first night.

The second day the nurse who taught our class asked if I would share a room with another patient. She also had gestational diabetes. She wasn't coping as well as me and Pollyanna. They felt it would be good to put us together for mutual support. We actually had the same specialist.

In hind sight, it was interesting that there were no other gestational diabetic patients in the hospital. We didn't live in a small town. It was curious that we just happened to have the same specialist. Was it possible we were the only two in the city? I was the obedient student in our class. I was eager to please and did everything they asked. My roommate didn't need anyone's approval and questioned everything they told her to do.

I had refused to let Scarlett come with me to the hospital because her attitude of worrying about things later helped put me in the hospital. I was giving myself shots, taking classes, and meeting with dieticians.

The only thing I didn't worry about was our two sons. I knew my husband could take care of them as well as I could. I worried about our unborn child; I needed Pollyanna, not Scarlett.

We were told the measures we were taking would keep our babies' glucose levels from dropping dangerously low during birth. Although I had not been conscientious about my own health through the years, or maybe because of that, I was over the top when it came to the wellbeing of my babies.

The moment I discovered I was pregnant, I stopped smoking and alcohol did not cross my lips. Aches and pains were endured because aspirin was not an option during pregnancy. After that first wakeup call from my OB, I took it easy when he said, take it easy and I went on bed rest when he said bed rest. I didn't like my specialist, but I was going to follow her instructions. Pollyanna was in control.

My roommate and I kept in touch after leaving the hospital. We compared notes and commiserated with each other. In the last month, she changed doctors. She called to tell me her new specialist was shocked at the amount of insulin she (and I) was taking. He cut her dosage by more than half and had a very different approach to treating gestational diabetes.

I could tell she was concerned and trying to give me a heads up, but Pollyanna was still in control. I wondered why there was such a difference in treatment; how could we know who was right? My OB asked how my numbers were running during a checkup; I showed him my glucose log. I sensed something concerned him because he asked if I was supposed to be keeping my sugar levels so low.

His reaction made me wonder, but Pollyanna said, "He wouldn't have sent you to a specialist if he felt comfortable treating it himself." When our third son was born, I figured out that there were no set rules for treating gestational diabetes. There were only best guesses and experiments because they had just recently started testing for the condition. There were doctors specializing in diabetic care, but there were no specialists treating gestational diabetes at the time.

Our third son's glucose levels did drop DANGEROUSLY LOW when he was born. They did have to give him IVs right away. The **specialist** wasn't there nor did she call, let alone check on us bedside. I do hope she got enough experience practicing on us to help future patients avoid the same situation.

The diabetic education nurse didn't get the warmest reception from me. At least she had the nerve and decency to come and see me. She had no explanation for what had HAPPENED. The very thing I jumped through flaming hoops to avoid, happened. Thankfully, roommate had made the right choice, her baby had no problems.

Looking back I realized the nurse, was only following doctor's orders. She was actually a very nice woman who was just doing her job. It was hard to understand what had gone wrong. As my OB said, I probably had gestational diabetes with the other two boys, but they didn't test for the condition back then.

I didn't have to see a specialist back then. I didn't have to take insulin back then. I didn't prick my finger seven times a day back then. My sugar levels never dropped dangerously low back then like they had several times during this pregnancy. And most of all, the first two babies were not born with dangerously low sugar levels *back then*. I wanted answers but no one had any to give.

Fortunately, the hospital staff and our wonderful pediatrician took care of our son quickly and efficiently. The worst thing was wondering if there would be long term health issues resulting from the treatment we received for gestational diabetes. Even after all these years, I wonder if it speeded up the onset of my Type II Diabetes or if it played a role in my son's health issues.

The only upside, if there is an upside to gestational diabetes, in most cases the disease disappears immediately after the baby is born. The downside, mothers are at higher risk for Type II Diabetes. I got the upside immediately and the downside later.

XIII

TIME TO WORRY

Since I had no way of knowing if there would be side effects, and since we got to bring our third beautiful son home, I ditched Pollyanna and made up with Scarlett. I would **worry *about it later.*** I wouldn't be having any more children, so there would be no more gestational diabetes. To decrease my chances of Type II, I would watch my weight, exercise, and eat right…later. As always, **later** came quicker than expected, five years later to be exact. Like my mother many years before, I started experiencing some classic diabetes symptoms. I talked with my OB. He did a blood test and said he would let me know the results.

On a beautiful sunny day Scarlett and I were taking the boys to the movies to see *The Lion King*. Excitement was in the air and the perfect picture of motherhood was on display. My handsome, well dressed sons were ready for the promised outing. I was dressed in a turquoise and white ensemble, looking tan and spiffy, if I do say so myself. Extra care had been taken because we were meeting Dad for a nice dinner after the movie.

My crisp cotton skirt had pockets full of tissues and candy. That day it was Tootsie Rolls. Forget popcorn and junior mints; I would be popping chocolate gooey goodness in my mouth as I watched the big screen. Tootsie Rolls get soft and chewy in a pocket next to a warm body!

We were going out the front door when the phone rang. Maybe it was Dad saying he could join us at the movie after all. I needed to find out because this took place back in the old days when leaving the house meant 'going dark' until you reached a hard wired phone. My husband had a mobile phone, but it was the size of a brief case and only used for business. I answered the old pick-up the receiver house phone.

"Hello . . . Yes, this is she." "I see; I was afraid of that. Who is he recommending? Good, because I would never use the SPECIALIST again under any circumstances." I hung up, took a deep breath, and said to the boy's expectant faces, "That wasn't Daddy, it was just my doctor's nurse calling." Not until that moment did I truly understand why I found Mom crying in the bathroom all those years ago.

If it hadn't been so close to show time, I would have gone to the bathroom for a private cry, but moms aren't made that way. Giving birth triggers the Spock Sacrifice in most women. I don't mean Dr. Benjamin Spock the well-known pediatrician. I'm talking about Mr. Spock from Star Trek, my all-time favorite show with my all-time favorite character. If Spock had not been Vulcan, he would have been German. The 'Spock Sacrifice' didn't happen in the TV show, it occurred much later in one of the 'made for the big screen' Star Trek movies.

Mr. Spock sacrifices himself to save the crew of the Starship Enterprise. His final words are, "The needs of the many, outweigh the needs of the few or the one." And that my friends is what every mom worth her salt does. She sacrifices her needs for the needs of her family. Oh sure, that concept didn't originate with Spock or with moms. We've just coined a cheap version from the originator himself, Jesus Christ. The one who did sacrifice for all.

...who does not need daily, as those high priests, to offer up sacrifices, first for his own sins, and then for the people's, for this He did once for all when He offered up Himself.
Hebrews 7:27 (NKJV)

Before my mom went to the bathroom for a good cry that morning, she got breakfast on the table and the family gears in motion. Then, and only then did she take some time for herself. So like my mom, instead of heading for the bathroom, I took the boys to the movie. Pollyanna was in full swing even though I was not *feeling ten feet tall* or **having a ball.**

I held it together and kept my promise. Scarlett and Polly helped; I was starting to enjoy the movie until... Simba's dad died. When that happened, I fell apart. I lost it so badly my youngest son leaned over to pat my arm and said, "It's OK Mom, it's just a cartoon." I wanted to say, "Yes honey I know it isn't real. I'm crying because I have diabetes."

I didn't say that because I had learned from experience. That information would have meant as much to them as it had to me all those years ago. Their questions would be different than mine were: Are we going to finish watching the movie? Will we still be meeting Daddy for dinner?

I let them think I was just upset over the movie. That was partially true; Mufasa's death did trigger my outburst. I guess my pony in that pile of manure was my having a good reason to cry. I looked sympathetic toward Simba instead of looking like a cry baby over a phone call.

You see, by that time I had already instilled the German psyche into my own sons. They didn't suffer crybabies any better than their great grandfather, their grandfather, or their mother. I didn't even think I had a right to cry. I had been warned for years, but never bothered to do anything about it. It was only a matter of time and time had run out.

I hadn't taken any steps to reduce my chances of getting diabetes. How could the boys understand how guilty and devastated I felt? Especially since Scarlett had already started to take control of the situation and I was popping Tootsie Rolls in my mouth as fast as I could. My syndrome allowed me to think, "I will eat chocolate today and worry about diabetes tomorrow."

When tomorrow came, I thought, "How could this have happened?" "How could I have diabetes?" "I'm not old!" Yeah, yeah, I know my risk factor was greater due to genetics and family history but...Yes, of course, I was well aware that I had gestational diabetes but...OK, so I'm a little overweight, but so are a lot of people who aren't diabetic. And just where do you get off bringing up my Tootsie Roll/Hershey Kiss addiction? Most women have chocolate cravings.

Exercise? How could any reasonable person expect me to find time to exercise? My busy schedule **was** exercise. I had cleaning, cooking, did two loads of laundry five days a week, and took three boys to school at two different locations. There was piano lessons, ice hockey, RA's, and Boys' Choir. I made sitting down to dinner a priority because other than chauffeuring, and Sunday sermons, I didn't get to sit much.

Once the boys were down for the night, I fell into bed hoping for a few hours of uninterrupted sleep. Sometimes our eldest couldn't sleep and wanted me to stay awake with him. Many nights my eyes automatically opened because I could sense him standing there, willing me to wake up.

On nights when Sweetest Heart had eaten something containing red dye, I was up cleaning. Most often it was cleaning him, his bed, his floor and his wall. Many times the only thing that didn't need to be cleaned between his room and the bathroom, WAS THE COMMODE. I'm a fairly frugal woman, but a couple of times it was cheaper to buy new pajamas and bedding instead of a new washer.

Stretch Armstrong Disease plagued The Baby. His growing pains were so severe we would massage his long legs until he could fall back to sleep. If by chance there was a peaceful night inside the house without one of the boys sleeping sideways in our bed, Argus, the family boxer took issue with something outside the house requiring human intervention. ME FINDING TIME AND ENERGY TO EXERCISE, REALLY?

Yes, really. I couldn't seem to find the time then? NOW, I had to find the time AND with all the same people, pets, and problems. The responsibilities and activities only increased through the years. If I had taken the time then, maybe I wouldn't have to make the time now. Do you feel my pain? Do you buy my excuses? Yeah, me neither. Lord, if I only had a do over.

> But You, O Lord, are a God full of compassion, and
> gracious, longsuffering and abundant in mercy and truth.
> **Psalm 86:15 (NKJV)**

How wonderful that we have a God of second chances. How totally amazing and blessed we are that He is also a God of third and fourth chances. How undeserving but necessary those chances are. That's because we quickly mess up the first, second, and third ones.

THANK YOU LORD! I was able to control my diabetes with diet. Oh wow, now I've learned my lesson. Now I will do things right. And I did...for a few years. Then I grew weary in well doing. I gradually began eating whatever I wanted and only exercised occasionally. Oh sure, I'd give myself a good talking to and do the right thing for a few days at a time. But there was never any long term changes.

Even though mom started out with diet control, she soon started taking oral meds and eventually became weary in well doing; she ended up on insulin injections. I told myself, that other than the inconvenience of shots, Mom was in pretty good shape. Since I wasn't even on oral medications, I had lots of years before I'd need injections, when I was old like Mom. Hello Scarlett, welcome home, you've been away for a while!

"The heart is deceitful above all things, And desperately wicked; Who can know it? I, the Lord, search the heart, I test the mind, Even to give every man according to his ways, According to the fruit of his doings."
Jeremiah 17:9&10 (NKJV)

XIV

SYMPTOMS

My sisters called to say Mom was in the hospital. It was her heart. Doctors said it was a complication from her diabetes. I had to make lots of arrangements for the boys and get to Kentucky. Wake-up Scarlett! Did you hear what my sister said? Diabetes really is the SILENT killer they say it is. Are things going wrong inside of me that I'm not even aware of?

Up until then, the only problem I was aware of from diabetes was an occasional yeast infection. You'd think that alone would be enough to make me keep my diabetes under control, right? But, women didn't have to go see a doctor to get prescriptions any longer. I could eat what I wanted to and worry about a yeast infection later. No big deal, medication was available over the counter now. Oh the tangled web we weave when first we practice to deceive…ourselves.

Who am I kidding, a yeast infection is always A BIG DEAL. But when it came to eating what I wanted and as much as I wanted, I turned to Scarlett. Anyway, I don't think there is actually a cure for a yeast infection. I suspect there are only placebos to make you think help is on the way. It helps you survive until the infection runs its' course. That's what I thought, but I still paid big bucks for the placebo. Every time, I hoped would be the time that relief would come quickly.

Back in the dark ages when a prescription was still needed, the nurse worked me in for a last minute appointment. You see, women couldn't be trusted to know if they had a yeast infection or not. I guess that was to prevent us from confusing a yeast infection with something life threating like a ruptured appendix or brain tumor.

I was at the doctor's office for the, (can't get a prescription without a) urine test. Another simple test, right? You're given a plastic cup the size of a thimble and told to collect a sample from mid-stream! MID-STREAM, are you kidding me? Maybe it was the same principle as not eating the first snow of the season.

Someone please tell me how to sanitarily collect urine from mid-stream. Even if I had enough control to start and stop, how is mid-stream calculated? Now? No, too early. How about now? No, not now. Now, should I try now? Oops, too late. Even if control and timing are on the money, you're still left with cup placement?

I headed to the restroom with my thimble. Ok, it wasn't actually the size of a thimble, but it was still smaller than a tiny juice glass. I suggested it would be easier if I just stuck my arm through the little metal sample door in the restroom wall. Then the nurse on the other side could just wipe the test strip over my hand; that's where most of the urine ended up.

The nurse insisted on following procedures so I hovered, timed, and aimed. I dried the cup, the commode seat, and sat the sample in the little door. Then, I thoroughly washed my hands. I came out and sure enough, the nurse was testing the sample she removed from the little door on the outside of the wall.

"My way would be easier," I said. We laughed and I started kvetching about having to come in instead of getting a prescription called to the pharmacy. She agreed and said, "Girl, you're preaching to the choir. If male doctors thought about using sandpaper on themselves, they would start calling in prescriptions." Yes mam, that woman had suffered.

I discovered a female doctor covering for my internal medicine guy had also suffered. I told her what over the counter treatment (a.k.a. placebo) I was using for a recurring infection, she said, "That's just making it mad. Here's something that will knock its lights out." Wow, she listened, understood, and fixed. I liked that woman.

Mom's hospital stay was long; one complication lead to another and another. She had dialysis three times because her kidneys were shutting down. It ended when she said, no more, take me home. We honored her wishes, took her home and prepared for her imminent passing. Mom lived two more years, but there wasn't much quality to her life. Could I be looking into my own future? I just had to get my diabetes under control.

Then a little voice began to whisper, "Maybe your mom's heart attack wasn't the result of diabetes. Maybe she just had a bad heart. Lots of people have heart attacks who aren't diabetic. Your dad died of a heart attack; he wasn't diabetic. Some doctors will automatically hang any symptom on the disease you have."

That's so true! It was a catch all. You could go to the doctor for hemorrhoids, and be told they were caused by your diabetes. It might run along these lines. Uncontrolled diabetes causes poor digestion. Poor digestion causes constipation. Constipation causes hemorrhoids. I went to the emergency room for severe back and leg pain one night and got a lecture about diabetes control. The doctor wasn't concerned with my excruciating pain from falling out of the choir loft. He was too busy chastising me to give any thought to something being seriously damaged.

I'm not kidding, he actually asked who my doctor was and said he would refuse to treat me if I was his patient. I was older and had previous experience (the Specialists) with his type. So I said, "I don't think there's the remotest possibility I would chose you for treating my diabetes. Is there anything you can do about the pain I have from falling?"

Yes, I fell out of the choir loft. It occurred one Sunday when we divided and moved to the side for a baptism. We did that so we could see the baptism and it kept the back row singers dry. I was standing at the end of the second row and was pushed next to the wall when we separated. That always made me a bit claustrophobic because I couldn't see anything with all the taller choir members surrounding me.

That day I noticed a large empty space on the row below me. Thinking the new girl had not moved all the way back, I decided to step down into that huge open space. I slowly stretched my left foot down…By the time I realized nothing was there, I lost my balance and Thump Ker Plunk!

New girl wasn't standing there because it was the space/pit where the side door opened into the risers. Singers who were near tried to help and discretely asked if I was Ok. I managed to stand up and assured them I was fine. That's when the shaking started. Not me, the sea of ivory robes trying to hold back laughter. They tried to regain control, but the congregation knew something funny happened. We were flooded with questions after that service.

That was the reason for my emergency room visit two days later. Scarlett made perfect sense when she suggested not all health issues are related to diabetes. It was possible Mom just had a bad heart. Hello Miss O'Hara, when did you get to Kentucky? I thought I left you back in Texas. What would I do without you?

Years passed before my A1C levels started to rise. My doctor suggested a new medication that was getting good results. It helped the limited insulin a Type II did produce to be more effective. One of the side effects was…weight loss. Hallelujah, Praise The Lord! Sign me up!

Alas, I did not lose any weight. Can't imagine why because food didn't stay in my system long enough to be stored as fat. I lost my social life and my dignity, but not a single pound of weight.

Certain foods were just incompatible with the medication. The moment the two collided, a convoy started in my stomach and headed for the nearest exit. It felt like eighteen wheelers driving through your lower intestine picking up speed at every turn. The food just jumped on board; no road block could stop it from reaching the final destination.

Following a monthly dinner with our church clique, we all headed to the mall for a movie. While waiting in the ticket line, the trucks started revving up in my stomach. I quietly said to my husband, "I need to go home. Let me have the keys." He asked why I was going home. "I don't feel well. You stay; I'll be back before the previews are over." My considerate husband said, "Let me get you a ginger ale to settle your stomach. It's probably just something you ate." **Trying** to be discreet I said, "It's my medication dear, I need my bathroom." Always the man with a better plan, he suggested the public restroom.

At that point my narrowing eyes said, "Really, you want to discuss my toilet preferences now?" He got the message, but was still clueless. "I'll just run you home," he said. By that time, through clinched teeth I said, "**Give me the keys and get a ride home**; I'm not coming back for you!"

If the other couples and other movie goers in the line hadn't figured out what was going on, it wasn't due to my husband's discretion. It wasn't one of my best moments. No one mistook me for a submissive Christian wife. I know several people who have experienced the same side effects; they back up my behavior that night.

That was the *first* time I tried the new miracle drug. I stopped because I needed to leave home occasionally. I did better with diet for a while, but eventually medication was necessary. I tried something different; it caused liver problems. I gave the miracle drug a *second* try by attempting to time food intake with location. That trial lasted a few months before I found something without side effects.

It worked well for several years before I reached maximum dosage. My doctor recommended trying the miracle drug with my current medication. *Third* time was charm, it worked. The miracle happened and I lost about ten pounds.

XV

OUT OF CHANCES

Two years ago the doctor said I was maxed out on my medication dosage and we should consider injections. I was a mess that day. As usual Scarlett was there to help and started to whisper. Instead of listening, I looked in the mirror and said, "Frankly Scarlett, I don't care anymore than Rhett did." Real friends don't lie.

> The righteous should choose his friends carefully,
> For the way of the wicked leads them astray.
> **Proverbs 12:26 (NKJV)**

I had a real friend who spoke truth, but I preferred hearing what I wanted to hear. He paid a great price for me, but I deposited the very minimum into our relationship. I knew of His great love and had accepted Him personally. He had blessed me over and over with mercy and grace. In return, I honored Him with obligation and words.

I thought about how honored I would feel if my children only checked in once a week out of duty and only visited on my birthday and Mother's Day. I know when something is done because of obligation and when it is done out of love. Did I think my Heavenly Father had less discernment than me?

He's glad when we show up on Sundays, or just for Christmas and Easter. He is honored when we show up at other times, just because we want to. We want our children's heart. So does God. He wants real fellowship and real relationships. I want to know my sons and do what I can to make that happen. Relationship, not obligation helps parents lead and guide from a position of love.

I realized there were areas of my life that did not honor God. I had been treating my body like a teenager often treats clothes, cars, or an education they didn't have to pay for themselves.

> Or do you not know that your body is the temple of the Holy Spirit who is in you, whom you have from God, and you are not your own? For you were bought at a price; therefore glorify God in your body and in your spirit, which are Gods.
> **1 Corinthians 6:19&20 (NKJV)**

I started exercising. The elliptical machine that decorated the exercise area was moved to the den. I literally had to step around it every day so I couldn't ignore it. I exercised while watching TV with my husband. I lost ten pounds and lowered my A1C levels. I had more energy and became more active. More activity gave me a better outlook. An improved outlook gave me the incentive to do something about other bad habits.

I admitted I had an addiction; I was using every day. Truth be told, I was using several times a day. Having a diet drink was the last thing I did before going to bed and the first thing I did every morning. I was seriously addicted to diet cola.

It started with regular colas, but due to the diabetes, I switched to the hard stuff. I was drinking two or three a day when a friend introduced me to zero cola. That was the beginning of my downward spiral.

I started carrying big purses to the movies to conceal my drink of choice and took my own to restaurants because they didn't have it in their soda fountains. I eventually kicked the zero habit but only by reverting back to diet cola. By then I was consuming more than a six pack a day.

Periodically I would go on a *no soft drinks at home* regimen. At restaurants, I could easily have two refills after sucking down the first 12 ounce glass. Still, not drinking them at home cut my consumption by a third.

One day I read an article saying you could lose ten pounds a year by giving up soft drinks. It went on to say, it didn't matter if you drank regular or diet soda regarding the weight loss. I decided to give it a try.

XVI

WEIGHT FOR IT

Three months after going off soft drinks cold turkey, I was still the same weight, but I felt better. The headaches and heartburn were gone so I stayed on the wagon. Giving them up was extremely difficult. I was a smoker years ago. Kicking that habit was a cake walk compared to giving up diet drinks.

I was truly addicted. I still long for that fizzy feeling in my mouth and the slow burn going down my throat. I know it would probably take drinking only one to get me hooked again. I even missed the explosive carbonation burps. I was able to stay on the wagon because I finally started noticing a little weight loss. I guess that was bound to happen eventually just from drinking more water.

I reached my first goal weight of not being morbidly obese. Of course I seldom saw myself as obese, except in pictures. I guess I suffered from the opposite of anorexia. People who suffer with that disease can't see their skeletal wasting bodies; they just see fat. I couldn't see fat, just pleasing plumpness.

Little doses of reality got through from time to time. When faced with photo reality, I would say, "Who hired the fat woman to stand in for me? Boy, the camera sure does add pounds." Sometimes I was surprised by department store windows. When I realized the reflection was me instead of another shopper, I wondered why windows had the same effect as cameras.

I've tried more weight loss plans than I can remember or care to discuss. If you have a weight problem, you already know about most of the plans. If you are not overweight or struggle to maintain a reasonable weight, YOU CANNOT POSSIBLY UNDERSTAND!

One day I was getting my hair done at my friend's salon. We eventually got around to discussing weight loss. We were chatting like close friends do when a svelte and stylish patron in the **station across the room** intruded to say, **If** we were serious about losing weight; she could help.

Why did Svelte feel the need to intrude? Being curious about what weight loss product she might be selling, I made a polite reply. Come to find out she had a six month old baby and had gotten back to her pre-pregnant weight in just three months. Big deal, I had kept weight off for three months several times myself.

Not to be rude, I smiled and made a proper response. The conversation was taking place through big mirrors in the front of each station. Svelte was gorgeous, so maybe she could help, although I wasn't thrilled with her snide comment about IF we were serious. Since I'm basically a nice person I feigned interest and asked, "How much weight did you gain during your pregnancy?"

OH NO! That poor woman. She had put on, are you ready for this? TWENTY SIX POUNDS! OH GROSS! Can you imagine letting yourself go like that? I started to ask if she had any 'before and after' pictures, but figured she probably did. I couldn't give her any more attention and just nodded with understanding.

I had run into her type before. The perfect size woman getting her validation from overweight women. You never know where they'll pop up. They can't just say 'no thank you' when offered something to eat. They can't remain silent during weight loss discussions between others. They take those opportunities to get their egos stroked.

"I wish I could eat that; I've just got to lose some weight," they say. Then wait for us to say, "You fat? NO WAY! You're perfect; I wish I looked like you." Let me just say here and now to women who have real struggles with weight, "STOP FEEDING THE FAT EGOS OF SKINNY WOMEN!"

My friend and I exchanged a knowing look in the mirror, the kind that speaks volumes. I had nothing to say at that point, absolutely nothing! My friend filled the silence by asking Svelte how she lost the weight. I could hardly wait to hear how a woman who never had a weight problem, managed to lose twelve to sixteen pounds after having a baby.

Svelte condescendingly told us that we would have to cut back on the amount of food we ate. The eye contact from my friend to me said, "I know that look, don't go there, this is my lively hood." My eye comment back was, "It might be your salon, but she is not your customer." Then out loud I said, "Did you hear that? Don't eat so much. If we had only known!"

Silence…awkward silence. All communication ceased except for the 'trying not to' smiles from almost everyone else in the salon.

That information should have been made available to everyone. You would think a doctor or nutritionist would have published a book or something. Just think of all the time and money wasted on diet plans that lets you eat as much of anything you want to eat. Bless Svelte's heart for being generous enough to share that revolutionary information. Now there was hope for us! Maybe one day we could be thin too.

I do owe Svelte an apology. Even though her motives were suspect, she was correct. No matter if it's counting calories, counting points, counting carbs, or counting fats, you won't lose weight until you eat less of the bad things and more of the good things.

Plus, losing weight after a ten pound gain, insures you won't have to face or overcome the challenges and problems associated with massive weight loss. To be honest, even if Svelt had been grossly overweight most of her life, her success story would not have inspired me. I was still searching for the easy way.

Years ago, I went to a 'miracle weight loss' doctor. A friend had great success with his plan. I lost forty pounds in about two and a half months without exercising. It was miraculous. All that was required was an appetite suppressant and eating about 500 CALORIES A DAY.

We were herded through his 'clinic' like cattle. Blood pressure was taken, we were weighed in by his obese nurse, then sent to his office to get berated. We were there just long enough for him to throw another 3 X 5 copy of his diet our way along with a fourteen day supply of pills. On the way out, he told us how many pounds to lose before returning in two weeks.

Like I said, there was no exercise! You didn't have to because you were so hyped up on the pills you couldn't sit still. I hated how I felt but...I was losing weight and our home was spotless!

The cars stayed washed, the yard stayed manicured. The garage, attic and closets were organized; no dust could be found on, under or behind the appliances. Neither potato chip nor loose change lived in our sofa cushions. The pantry held alphabetized can goods and crumbs lasted no longer than two days in the silverware drawer. I would iron sheets and pillow cases if I ran out of things to do.

Guess what I learned from that experience? Another name for appetite suppressant is SPEED and SPEED has a street value. Come to find out, you don't need exercise **or** sleep when taking Speed, and it's hazardous to your health. I also learned some doctors do not take the Hippocratic Oath seriously. And come to find out, when you eat less than is required to sustain life, YOU WILL LOSE WEIGHT even without exercise or appetite suppressants.

I discovered a dangerous way to lose weight, but not how to keep it off. I gained the weight back and a better understanding of Stockholm Syndrome. Doctor Dangerous had brain washed patients into believing he was helping them instead of his bank account.

Because of his outrageous demands, we wore our lightest clothes, took off our shoes, jewelry, and even shaved our legs before appointment weigh in. We hated him, but we kept giving him money to degrade us. I don't know what actuarial chart he used, but on my first visit he said, "Well Rhonda, it looks like you need to lose half of Rhonda."

I haven't tried **everything** to lose weight, but I have tried a lot: cabbage soup, fasting, grapefruit, protein shakes, water. My friends and I even tried hypnotism. I really wanted that to work. I just didn't respond well to the power of suggestion. After the first session, the hypnotist told us to go home and eat something we really enjoyed, something we usually ate too much of. He said that our desire for the food would be gone.

I was dubious. When we were supposed to be completely relaxed and under the power of suggestion, he said, "You are so relaxed, you can't raise your arm. Take a deep breath and try to raise your arm." I wanted it to work, but my arm came right up.

I went home and tried a chocolate kiss. My husband looked at me with anticipation and said, "Well?" When I finished savoring every bit of the luscious goodness, I said, "Maybe it will take eating the whole bag." That ended my hypnosis weight loss program.

XVII

WHAT WORKED

I *have* lost at least half of Rhonda through the years and found a larger version of her again and again. The only real success came from doing it slowly and healthfully. I'm not advocating any plan, but the only time I haven't gained back more weight than I lost, was with a popular long established weight loss program. I would join, lose ten to fifteen pounds, give up on reaching goal and quit. But, I never gained all the weight back.

This gave me a lower set point body weight each time. I was able to maintain a lower weight until I was motivated to try again. I did that three times over the years and finally reached a size (not a weight) that I was okay with.

I maintained that weight until my diabetes got worse along with my blood pressure and cholesterol. I was getting injections in my eyes due to diabetic retinopathy, and had started having some numbness in my feet. More medicine was not the answer. Medication wasn't even the easy way out any more.

I felt horrible, I looked horrible and I missed out on so much from just being sick from all the medication. Something had to be done.

I knew and had learned the hard way what needed to be done. Lose weight!

I took Svelte's advice and stopped eating so much. I had already cut out soft drinks, so I decided to cut back on the bread and began taking part of my eating out meals home for lunch the next day. I was raised to *waste not, want not*, so I couldn't just leave food on the plate. Then I found an app for my cell phone to track calories. It was very motivational and made me aware of how much I actually ate. Success at last!

Don't think for one minute I didn't go to the Great Physician for help through the years. I knew it had worked for others. I was a Christian. I knew He could help. I just didn't know if He would. I prayed, "Lord, please help me lose weight." "Lord, look at the damage I'm doing." "Please Lord, in Jesus name I pray." I gave my best arguments and even used the secret words, *in Jesus name,* to no avail.

If you ask anything in My name, I will do it.
John 14:14 (NKJV)

Why didn't it work? Should I have gone to Him first? Did my obvious disrespect for the temple in the past indicate I needed more time in the refining fire? Maybe I should have sought His advice instead of His fix? In hind sight, praying for the skills to keep my body healthy might have been more helpful than praying for a beautiful body.

I get it! Now I'm finally getting it. I don't have all the answers and never will. But I am **learning**. The advice and counsel I needed had been there all along. It boils down to this. Go to Him first. Pills and an easy way are temporary and often damaging. Don't ask Him to fix the things that He gives you the tools to fix yourself. Respect your body, something very special should be residing there. And, examine the motives for your request. Having a body your husband finds attractive is quite different than wanting a body everyone finds attractive. Praying for a healthy body is a far cry from praying for a sexy body.

God wasn't saying no to my prayers for losing weight. He was saying wait, not now. You don't have what it takes to handle it, **yet**.

He was right of course. I didn't have what it took to handle it. I truly believe if I had prayed for the strength and maturity to handle losing weight for the right reasons, my prayers would have been answered sooner and a lot of damage could have been avoided. Remember, how long it takes to learn basically depends on you.

I'm finally at a weight I never dreamed possible, just slightly over-weight. All things **are** possible with God. I have stopped using one of my diabetic medications and cholesterol medication. I haven't had eye injections or laser treatments in over a year. I feel so much better. I *feel* my age, but I've felt this age for fifteen years. I wish it had not taken so long to get here.

I regret the damage I've done, especially the gestational diabetes that might have been avoided. I will always feel guilty over a quick fix diet that made emergency gall bladder surgery necessary. I have no way of knowing for sure, but suspect the surgery played a role in hurting someone else. It's a thorn I carry. Like Paul's thorn in his flesh, I plead with the Lord to remove it, but concerning this thing…

…He said to me, "My grace is sufficient for you, for My strength is made perfect in weakness." Therefore most gladly I will rather boast in my infirmities, that the power of Christ may rest upon me.
2 Corinthians 12:9 (NKJV)

I'm not Paul, so I brood instead of boast about the thorn, about my failures, and about my shortcomings from time to time. But, only long enough to get a good dose of reality when I start to playing in the fire again.

But I will hope continually, And will praise
You yet more and more.
Psalm 71:14 (NKJV)

Losing focus means gaining weight and diminished joy. Gaining weight means health complications and insulting the Lord who gave me another chance. I can't do anything about what's in the past, but I can do better in the future. I concentrate on the narrow gate. The broad gate leads to destruction. There's too much space for food, drink and bad habits at the broad gate. It leads to damage to ourselves, our loved ones and those we witness to.

"Enter by the narrow gate; for wide is the gate and broad is the way that leads to destruction, and there are many who go in by it. Because narrow is the gate and difficult is the way which leads to life, and there are few who find it."
Matthew 7:13&14 (NKJV)

THE NARROW GATE

☙☙

XVIII

THE TEST

Replacing the fiction of SOPS with reality was a long time coming. I had grown in lots of ways: length, width, and depth. I had emotional stability, mental acuity, educational knowledge, and spiritual awareness. But, I lacked focus.

Focus means narrowing, as on a target. You can't achieve marksman status without it. It takes more than raising a gun and pulling the trigger. Anyone can be a shooter, but it takes focus to hit the target. It takes practice **and** focus to hit the bull's eye. I needed to at least start hitting the target. If I wanted to get through the narrow gate, I had to start focusing on it.

Growing in faith happens when we are tested. At some point in our walk with the Lord, we realize the testing won't end until we are with the Lord. Sounds like a bummer doesn't it? We whine and moan. Why Lord? Not again Lord. How many times Lord? Then one day we realize God is not the one testing. He is the one providing the answers to the test, and He is the one who will grade it!

> In this you greatly rejoice, though now for a little while, if
> need be, you have been grieved by various trials...receiving

the end of your faith-the salvation of your souls.
1 Peter 1:6&9 (NKJV)

My high school government teacher gave a test every Friday. On Thursday he wrote the test questions on the board. At some point during class, he would erase them. And still, some students failed his class?

Christians often behave like that senior government class. Several automatically wrote the questions down to study. Some procrastinators scribbled frantically as the questions were being erased (that was me/Scarlett). The smart ones read the questions and just wrote down the ones they couldn't answer. Sadly, a few did nothing at all.

No one wants to fail. But many do, even when the answers are on the board or in the Bible. Why? Free time was great until grades and graduation approached. Our government teacher didn't give second chances, fortunately God does.

He's a God of multiple chances, but not unlimited chances. He is patient and limitless, but He does give us limits. Never confuse God's patience with His acceptance. There are Biblical gray areas open to interpretation. I think those areas are by divine design.

Our government teacher always had a few questions that did not show up on the test. I can only speculate that he felt it would be good for us to have those answers, but our grade did not depend on them. Maybe the same is true for God's gray areas.

Since there are many areas open to interpretation, shouldn't we at the very least try to live according to what is spelled out **in black and white** and **chiseled in stone**? We can't live according to what is right in our own eyes. Where is the honor in that? We can't make a passing grade by answering questions that are not on the test. You might get extra credit for them, but not enough to pass.

Some of us have to lose a lot or all before realizing we've focused on the wrong questions or the wrong gate. Remember the old 'Let's Make A Deal' game show? Some contestants passed on $10,000 behind door number one, hoping for a new car behind door number two. They made decisions based on what was right in their own eyes. They went home with a donkey! Wanting too much blinds us from what we really need.

I'm not going to fret about the length of my journey or the many times I've been a donkey. Instead, I'll celebrate getting multiple chances. Getting there later is better than not getting there. It took the disciples a while to work through and understand who Jesus was, and they were physically with Him day after day. They saw His miracles and knew His character, yet missed the mark in the beginning. And, one tragically missed it altogether.

I don't have percentages, but have been told there's a greater chance of accepting Christ when you're young. Why not when you are older? Some of the reasons are: getting set in your ways, feeling too intelligent to fall for the hoax, or seen too many bad Christian examples.

I find the intelligence excuse interesting. Many who use that excuse have never even read the Bible. Although being *well read* is not a requirement for intelligence, you'd think intelligent people would at least give the best seller of all time a cursory read? There are a great many classics I have not read, but THE best seller of all time is not one of them.

What about the bad Christian example excuse? If you've read the best seller, you would have discovered the only example we are to follow is that of Jesus Christ. Christians are not perfect, they're forgiven.

The *set in your ways* excuse causes me the most concern; it's a dangerous place to sit! Old dogs refusing to learn new tricks. I've known many who even take pride in being obstinate; that's sad and pitiful.

Toddlers get away with being stubborn and strong willed, not mature adults. That's just advertising senility or not being intelligent enough to learn.

No matter how many dues you have paid or think you have paid, you haven't earned the right to behave like a spoiled child. I know the importance of reaching our youth. What about those who are short on time and running out of chances?

The Bible tells us that when Judas realized what he had done, he was heartbroken. He tried to return the silver, and was remorseful. Did he ask for forgiveness; would he get a second chance? Was he too ashamed to ask? Did he understand that he could? Other disciples failed Jesus and went on to become martyrs of the faith. What happened with Judas?

Men with shortcomings were responsible for spreading the gospel throughout the world. Peter denied Jesus three times and became the rock on which the Church was built. Would God have forgiven Judas or had he reached his limit? Can we even compare betrayal with missing the mark a few times?

Will you get another chance? Will you kick your destructive habits? Most importantly, will you find salvation? I believe as long as we have breath, we have hope. Your life may be a mess, but it doesn't have to stay that way. It can be better, healthier, and more joyful! You can still avoid the worst consequence, an eternity separated from the love of God. And you can be reunited with your earthly family who did find salvation.

Living the rest of your allotted days for Him here on earth is a blessing. If you have never been good at learning from the mistakes of others, make an exception and learn from Judas. Ask for forgiveness.

I've made a lot of messes in my life, especially where my health was concerned. I've corrected course, but the consequences remain.

Correcting course does not equate into Do Overs. No one gets a do over, but we often get a try again. It's another chance for the future, not changing what happened in the past. Don't make the mistake of thinking it's too late. Use what you have learned from the past and TRY AGAIN.

XIX

SALVATION

I was saved at a revival when I was a senior in high school. Two young preachers were holding a revival in a nearby community. Many of us attended because it was our social outlet. Our parents would say no to concerts, movies, parties, and ball games from time to time. But never church, even on school nights.

We were there to connect, to see and be seen. Most of the service was spent glancing at certain boys in the church and trying to see which ones were standing outside the church. There was always a chance one would offer to drive or walk us home.

Letting a boy walk us home wasn't as risky as getting in a car, but we still had to be careful. Parents always found out who did the walking. A lot of 'sparking' got done on those walks home from churches that were just a little piece down or up the road.

Something was different about the service that night. I was listening to the sermon instead of enduring it. We were good at enduring because getting up for a restroom break was frowned upon. If you couldn't control your bladder long enough to sit through a sermon, you might have to stay home.

I'm strict about using the restroom as an excuse to run back and forth. I didn't let my boys do it, and my grandson hasn't tried. I know it's only a matter of time. But if he has bladder control at three, what are the chances I'll let him leave the service when he's older? Occasionally is to be expected; often is a bad habit or a bad bladder.

Friday night was our regular church night. I suspected that day was chosen to keep us away from football games. Other churches had different church nights; some were Saturday and some Sunday. Maybe it was a conspiracy to keep us from having any weekend fun. Most church decisions seemed to be made by pious, judgmental, narrow minded people. Oh don't be shocked, teens always think the world revolves around them.

I don't know how or when it happened, but I became one of those narrow minded old folks. My constant battle is making sure my heart is broad enough to make up for the narrowness of my mind. Telling others how to live and what to do comes easy. Even when I manage to control my tongue, my face makes up for what my mouth isn't saying, and I am seldom at a loss for words.

I went back to get my degree in psychology when The Baby started first grade. I switched majors when I discovered I preferred telling people what to do instead of helping them discover what they should do. I thought my way was quicker, easier, and a lot cheaper.

When I took the spiritual gifts test, I scored highest in admonition and lowest in mercy. I'm an opinionated, judgmental old church lady, but I'm getting better. I've been in God's refining fires a long time. I would like to think He just has some final polishing to do, but whether the polishing cloth or the fire, I'm thankful He's still working on me.

I like giving my opinion so much, I have contemplated writing a book on proper church etiquette. It would cover such topics as:

Church Attire-It should cover enough flesh to keep you comfortable in a sixty degree room and loose enough to hide whether your belly button is an innie or an outie.

Cell Phones-They should be on silent or off. The William Tale Overture can be funny during general announcements, but a grieving family is seldom amused when it goes off during the eulogy.

Texting-Don't do it unless a mad man has taken over the church and you need to contact the authorities.

Sleeping In Church-Nodding off in the choir loft can be overlooked, snoring and drooling cannot.

Church Math-If twenty three people are going through the 'pot luck' lunch line with twenty three pieces of chicken on the platter, how many pieces of chicken should you put on your plate?

ONE FOR CRYING OUT LOUD, just ONE!

Unfortunately, this lesson needs to be reinforced. If there are a dozen doughnuts for your Sunday School Class of ten, can each person have two doughnuts?

NO, NO THEY CAN'T.

The Sanctuary-It's holy treat it that way.

Food and Beverages-Both belong in the kitchen, in fellowship hall or on the grounds.

Animals-Exceptions could probably be made for the seeing impaired but otherwise, keep animals at home or in the nativity scene.

A dear sweet sister alerted me to the fact that the dog under a pew belonged to a seeing impaired woman instead of an overindulgent pet owner. Otherwise, a very awkward conversation might have taken place.

Church Commerce-Not in the sanctuary no matter whose child is raising money for cheerleading, band, dance, a sports team or a mission trip.

I'm not saying you would be turning God's house into a den of thieves. I don't have that kind of authority. I just think if Jesus got angry enough to turn tables over in the outer courts, shouldn't we at least keep buying and selling out of the sanctuary.

Offering Plates-Use them for tithes and offerings. The look on an usher's face when you chase him down to make change is hilarious, but very inappropriate.

Prayer Requests-Know the difference between a request and whining.

Keep them simple. If your request begins with: My sister's father-in-law's cousin's neighbor fell coming out of that grocery store that's on the street next to the library and broke the little bone connected to his...THAT'S NOT SIMPLE!

Praises-There's a difference between praising and bragging, figure it out.

Restroom Breaks-Except for emergencies and the bladder impaired, going to the restroom should take place before or after church.

I could have saved myself the most embarrassing moment of my life if I had only applied the restroom rule to other church events. I was asked to be one of the speakers for our church's building campaign dinner. I agreed and was excited that the banquet was taking place at my alma mater, Dallas Baptist University.

That night hundreds from our congregation gathered in the Great Hall to enjoy dinner, special music, and hearing heart felt hopes for the future of our church. I was feeling proud of my church, my school and my family. The difference in feeling proud and feeling blessed depends on who gets the credit. I must have got confused.

> When pride comes, then comes shame;
> But with the humble is wisdom.
> **Proverbs 11:2 (NKJV)**

I went to the restroom after dinner. When I heard the music preceding my time to speak, I said a quick prayer, checked for food in my teeth, freshened my lipstick, fluffed my hair, and headed back to my seat. I maneuvered quickly to a tale in the front of the room to the right of the podium.

I had just settled primly in my seat when my eldest got up from his table and came toward me. That in itself was cause for concern because he would never call unnecessary attention to himself. He leaned over and whispered, "Mom, word passed down through the room that your dress is tucked in your pantyhose."

My heart started sending blood to my face at an alarming rate. I was sweating and the room started spinning. "Ok Rhonda, calm down. Maybe just a bit of your flowy dress got snagged." I reached back and gave a little tug only to discover it was necessary to raise up off the seat and pull a huge portion of dress out of my hose. I had just flashed half the room with half my derriere. Especially since 'pantyhose' meant exactly that to me, panties and hose. "Lord if you love me, let the Rapture happen now."

He did not sweep me up to heaven. Instead, He gave me the courage to go to the podium and apologize for getting attention in such an unorthodox way.

I talked about giving to the future of our church and sat down with sadness because I wouldn't be a part of that future. I would be looking for a new church home where no one knew my name or at least hadn't seen my backside.

Humor came to the rescue. Most of the people thought my apology was an opening joke. When I told them it wasn't a joke and had actually just happened, they laughed even harder. Humor covers a multitude of awkward situations. You've got to love people who find a way to laugh with you instead of at you.

Only a few actually witnessed my shame. Bless them for passing the information down the room. It saved complete humiliation because I would have flashed the other half of the room leaving the podium. It wasn't the same as Noah's sons covering his nakedness, but it was along those same lines. You can't desert people who try to cover your nakedness.

I would have been better off not taking that trip to the restroom. The closest I ever came to leaving an actual sermon occurred when I was a teenager. Our pastor preached a short sermon before asking a visiting preacher if he had a word for us.

The teens sat on the back right pews. Every group had a spot: deacons sat stage left, choir stage right, the amen corner was left front, older women on the right, older men on the left, and a few young married couples sat together.

When preachers made comments about short skirts, long hair, fast cars, or rock'n roll, we could step on each other's toes, our way of saying this sermon is for you. When the visiting preacher went to the pulpit, we chanced a knowing look at each other. We liked that sweet old gentleman. But, he was long winded and we were anxious to go to someone's house and watch Chiller or play Rook.

He opened with these words, "I'm going to preach from Revelation on the Seven Seals." Another look passed between the teens. I don't know when I zoned out, but one hour later my bladder brought me back to consciousness hearing these words, "Now, to the Fifth Seal." I don't know how, but I managed to stay put instead of going to the restroom.

At my current age, I have friends who would dearly love to sit through an entire sermon without going to the restroom. That's why I'm trying to be more understanding since my time for bladder control issues may not be that far away.

I don't recall the message or the length of the sermon the night I was saved. I just recall the urge to go to the front. Something in me was different. I knelt at the altar and prayed the sinner's prayer, but I didn't experience the 'shouting and praising' that I witnessed in some new converts. Was I really saved? I thought so.

I felt saved before I went to my knees. It came to me in the anonymity of a packed church. It gave me the courage to stumble over others in the pew as I rushed to make my decision public.

Maybe the shouting and praising would come at the baptism. The following Sunday, guess how I came up out of the river? NOPE, the same as when I went in, quiet and subdued. But, I had peace knowing I would spend eternity with Jesus.

Was I really saved back then? I would ask myself that question through the years. I knew God loved me. I acknowledged Jesus died for me. I accepted the gift of salvation. Could it actually be that simple? Yes, it's really that simple. The more I know Him, the more I love Him and the more I want to TRY and repay that 'almost too good to be true deal' He gave me.

I mess up less now than I did back then, but that doesn't make Him love me more. Hallelujah, He doesn't love me less when I do mess up, because I will mess up. My sanctification was, is and will continue to be an ongoing process.

I can't repay the debt I owe, the blood of Jesus had to settle it. But I make an effort to live as though I could. Completely IMPOSSIBLE, but still a good goal to focus on. I'm happiest when I have a goal. I spent the first twenty years of my life making an effort for my earthly father. He couldn't have loved me anymore or any less than he did the day I was born, neither does our Heavenly Father. Even when we are wrong, weak, and weary.

Did I disappoint him? You bet I did, but disappointment isn't connected to love. Making the effort for my Heavenly Father wasn't automatic, it took time, soul searching, and effort. And it has been worth it because…

Blood is thicker than water. Thankfully, I was born into the right family both times. THE BLOOD OF JESUS COVERS ALL.

FINAL THOUGHTS

You've probably got a glimpse of my self-centered psyche through the pages of this book. That's why you won't be surprised when I say *Thicker than Water* was written for me. It didn't start out that way. I wanted it to be an entertaining way to encourage others and I hope it did. But, I've learned through the years that when I'm doing for others, I'm the one who gets the most blessings.

I teach a wonderful group of ladies in Sunday School. They are very encouraging and appreciative, but I'm the one who gets the most from preparing the lesson. Writing this book has been no different. I'm the one who has benefited most. God has spoken to me in wondrous ways through the course of the writing. I pray He spoke to you through the reading.

If the bad in your life outweighs the good, focus on the good. If you can't find the good, stop looking back and start looking up. As a child, sunlight was my armor. As an adult, Son-light is my armor. I hope my struggles with faith, weight and diabetes help you or at least keep you searching until you can find the right armor to fight the good fight.

> And so find favor and high esteem in the sight of God and man. Trust in the LORD with all your heart, And lean not on your own understanding; In all your ways acknowledge Him, and He shall direct your paths.
> **Proverbs 3:4-6 (NKJV)**

To God be the glory...

ABOUT THE AUTHOR

R.C. Tuttle considers herself blessed to be a Kentucky Hillbilly and privileged to be a naturalized Texan. Mother to three sons of the Lone Star State, she lives with her husband in their 'empty nest' home located in the Dallas/Fort Worth Metroplex. Mrs. Tuttle retired as headmaster of a Christian school and now teaches Sunday School, writes, and speaks to women's groups and organizations.

Printed in the United States
By Bookmasters